How to pray for healing, freedom and deliverance

by

Dr Liz Hill O'Shea

Copyright © 2024 by Liz Hill-O'Shea All rights reserved.

Published in the United Kingdom by author:

Dr Liz Hill-O'Shea

All scripture quotations, unless otherwise indicated, are taken from the Holy Bible, New International Version®, NIV®.

Copyright ©1973, 1978, 1984, 2011 by Biblica, Inc.™ Used by permission of Zondervan. All rights reserved worldwide. *www. zondervan.com*

The "NIV" and "New International Version" are trademarks registered in the United States Patent and Trademark Office by Biblica, Inc.™

Also by this author:

10 Steps to Knowing God: A Discipleship Guide to Developing an Intimate Relationship with God for Small Groups and Personal Devotions

Running with God: A Discipleship Guide to Grow in Faith and Experience the Power and Love of God

The Nature of Faith and Miracles: How to Experience God's Power and Purpose

Born for a Purpose: Finding God's Purpose for Your Life

Journal for Animal Lovers: with Bible Verses and Colouring Pages

Contents

Part A: Prayer and the role of the Holy Spirit 5

Chapter 1: Benefits of prayer 7
Chapter 2: Praying in the Holy Spirit 27
Chapter 3: God speaks by His Holy Spirit 49

Part B: Praying through the Lord's Prayer 65

Chapter 4: Our Father in Heaven, Hallowed be
Your name 67
Chapter 5: Your kingdom come. Your will be done
on earth as it is in heaven 79
Chapter 6: Give us this day our daily bread 99
Chapter 7: And forgive us our debts, as we forgiven
our debtors 123
Chapter 8: And do not lead us into temptation,
but deliver us from the evil one 141

Part C: Pray for healing and deliverance 169

Chapter 9: How to pray for healing 171
Chapter 10: Freedom from curses 201
Chapter 11: How to pray for deliverance: Five Steps
to freedom 213
Chapter 12: For yours is the kingdom and the power
and the glory forever 229
Chapter 13: Continue to grow in God 237

Introduction

God wants to set you free! He wants to bring the necessary inner, physical or spiritual healing you know you need but have not yet understood how to obtain.

This book will help you with that, taking you on a journey towards health and wellbeing as God intends. Prayer is an important instrument of that process. Praying to almighty God is not only one of the greatest privileges and blessings we have in life. It is also the most effective and powerful thing you can do for yourself and your loved ones because God will move miraculously in answer to your prayers.

Prayer is essentially communicating with God and asking for His help and intervention, no matter how impossible a need appears. It's done in the context of a relationship with God, who loves and cares for you and invites you to draw near to Him. God has a wonderful purpose for your life and bringing healing and freedom from what holds you back is an important part towards fulfilling that.

Nothing is impossible with God

In my pastoral ministry experience, I have met many people who were struggling with all sorts of problems from physical sickness, depression and anxiety to mental or spiritual torment, and who didn't know how to find freedom. This book has been written in response to these needs. You will learn how praying in the name of Jesus Christ, led by the

Holy Spirit and the Word of God will bring the healing and freedom you need.

Some churches teach their members that God uses their unresolved suffering to simply forge their faith and character and nothing more. Whilst the Bible does indeed teach that God uses our suffering to draw us closer to Him, it also teaches that God wants to deliver us from all our troubles. God wants to answer your prayers and bring the divine help you long for. God can do for you what no medical specialist can do. Nothing is impossible to God.

As followers of Christ, seeing God move miraculously in and through our lives is meant to be the norm. We are not meant to live powerless lives, overcome by our problems and sicknesses, slowly having our days stolen from us. We have been given many great promises from God in the Bible on the subject of healing, freedom, deliverance, divine provision and guidance, enabling us to be overcomers who walk in faith and victory in Christ. That's what the Lord's Prayer is all about.

Powerful promises

In the Bible, Jesus made some very great promises to those who turn to God in prayer:

> "If you believe, you will receive whatever you ask for in prayer." Matthew 21:22.

> "Therefore I tell you, whatever you ask for in prayer, believe that you have received it, and it will be yours." Mark 11:24.

Was Jesus not sincere when He gave these promises? Of course He was! Given these magnificent promises, it would therefore be prudent to pray. God always keeps His promises. *Always.* The problem is, we often just don't know how to appropriate them. This book will teach you how.

Unlimited reach

Prayer has the power to change the lives of anyone you pray for, whoever they are. It's one of the most important and effective things you can do as a follower of Jesus Christ. It's not just an invitation; it's an expectation and even a command from God. The Bible says, "When you pray…" not "if you pray…". A prayerless life is a powerless life.

In your private place of prayer, you can pray and ask for God's divine power and intervention for anything, anyone and anywhere. You can literally change the world through your prayers because Jesus promised that if you pray and believe, God will answer and you will see great miracles.

This book will teach you how to engage in this great privilege of prayer and see God move powerfully in your life. Towards this goal, we will first look at what prayer is and its importance, then move on to look at the power and teaching of the Lord's Prayer, after which we will learn how to pray for healing, freedom and deliverance. Believe what God can do for you:

> "Now to him who is able to do far more abundantly than all that we ask or think, according to His power that is at work within us, to him be glory in the church and in Christ Jesus throughout all generations, forever and ever. Amen." Ephesians 3:20-21

So are you ready to begin your journey to healing? Let's begin.

Part A

Prayer and the role of the Holy Spirit

Chapter 1

Benefits of prayer

"Early in the morning, as Jesus was on his way back to the city, he was hungry. Seeing a fig tree by the road, he went up to it but found nothing on it except leaves. Then he said to it, 'May you never bear fruit again!' Immediately the tree withered.
When the disciples saw this, they were amazed. 'How did the fig tree wither so quickly?' they asked.
Jesus replied, 'Truly I tell you, if you have faith and do not doubt, not only can you do what was done to the fig tree, but also you can say to this mountain, 'Go, throw yourself into the sea,' and it will be done. If you believe, you will receive whatever you ask for in prayer.'"
Matthew 21:18-22.

Prayer can heal our wounded world

Prayer moves God, and when God moves, miraculous things happen. Life with Jesus Christ is meant to be a display of God's good works, which will draw people to Him. We are called to walk in God's power, revealing God's love and grace to a wounded world in desperate need of hope and healing. Prayer is the means that brings God's power down from heaven to earth, changing your life and the lives of those you pray for.

This is all possible because of Jesus Christ. He came to destroy the works of Satan (1 John 3:8) and save and heal a hurting and lost world. It should be straightforward to recognise the handiwork of Satan. Jesus said the enemy, Satan, came to steal, kill and destroy, whilst He came to give us life to the full (John 10:10). The work will reveal the author behind it. Anything that does not lead to life is not from God.

When Jesus Christ died on the cross and rose from the dead, Christ defeated and disarmed Satan (Colossians 2:15) and secured victory for us all. Following His ascension back to the Father, Christ entrusted His Church with His mission to implement His victory to save and heal our hurting world. As a result, we can apply Christ's victory over every kind of evil and suffering through prayer.

We are called to walk in victory, not defeat.

Through prayer in the name of Jesus Christ, God continues to bring salvation, healing and deliverance into people's lives, overcoming all the power and works of the evil one, just as Christ did when He walked this earth.

Jeremy and Scala are one couple who have dedicated their lives to God's mission work. As they share the gospel and pray for the sick, they have seen God work miraculously, bringing transformation and healing into people's lives. Here is one of their many stories of how God worked through their prayers on a mission trip in South India:

> We had stopped on the side of the road in a very small village in the middle of nowhere. That day we only had one translator, but there were twelve of us trying to share the gospel. We finished our programmes of worship dances, dramas, and preaching and praying for the sick.

As I looked around, I saw some ladies and a small baby. My friend and I approached the group and tried to talk, but they didn't speak English. They motioned to the baby, letting us know she was sick. The poor little baby was very hot when we touched her. We put our hands on her and prayed, and when we finished, she seemed to be healed. Then the grandmother, who was sitting next to the baby and was also sick, wanted prayer. We prayed for her, and she was healed too. They took us into the nearby house where the great grandmother was sitting down. She had knee pain and was pointing for us to pray. So we did, and afterward she stood up, kicked her knee and laughed. She too was healed! By now we desperately wanted to share more deeply about Jesus, but our only translator was busy. Instead, we just shared the gospel with them in English.

When we finished, one of the ladies started to point to the Hindu red dot that was on her forehead. I didn't understand, but I saw the translator was now free. We brought him over, and he started to share the gospel. Soon they stopped him and said that they understood everything we shared with them the first time. What they wanted to know was, since they now believed in Jesus, did they still need to wear the Hindu dot? Praise God! Even though we didn't speak their language, the Holy Spirit helped them hear His message in a way they could understand."

Through their prayers, these people received miraculous healings. Because they were touched by the power and love of God, their hearts became open to learning more about the God who healed them. When people who do not yet know God see Him touch their lives, it opens hearts wide. It creates a hunger to know who this powerful and loving

God is and leads them to salvation. Prayer is so powerful and effective.

I live in the United Kingdom and there's not a great deal of interest in following God here. However, whenever my husband does outreach on the streets and prays for people, they are amazed when they are healed. They are then willing to listen when he shares the gospel message of Christ and how much God loves them.

If you believe, you will receive

In Matthew 21, we read how Jesus cursed a fruitless fig tree so that it would never bear fruit again. It seems a bit strange that Jesus would do this, but from His following dialogue, it becomes clear that He was using it as a teaching point: "If you believe, you will receive whatever you ask for in prayer." As you stand on Christ's promises, you will see God do wonderful miracles through your prayers. There are just so many benefits to prayer as I've experienced in my own life. I'll share a few examples here of answered prayer.

Bone regrowth

After a dental x-ray about four years ago, my dentist informed me that the bone around my teeth in my lower jaw was receding. He didn't understand the reason why as I keep my teeth in good condition. He put it down to aging and informed me that I needed to be careful with my teeth to slow down the receding process. He explained how at my age (I was in my late forties at the time), bone doesn't regrow, and it was likely that my teeth would become looser in their sockets as time went by. I could feel that one or two were already a little lose and so when I heard this, I was concerned and decided I would pray and ask God for healing. So that is what I did. For the next two years, I prayed on and off that God would regrow the bone around my teeth in my lower jaw. I prayed for a creative miracle, and in the name of Jesus Christ, prayed for the bone to regrow.

Two years later it was time for my next x-ray on my jaw to see how things were progressing. The dentist said, 'I don't know how, but the bone has regrown around your teeth!' I was thrilled to hear this and told him it was an answer to prayer. God cares about the smallest things.

Healing from negative Covid vaccination reaction

After having my first Covid vaccination, I suffered a somewhat frightening reaction. After a month or so following the injection, my heart literally felt like a rock in my chest after I exercised. This began happening every time I exercised and it was quite concerning to say the least. What would that mean for my life? Would I ever be able to exercise again? I didn't think the doctor could do anything to heal me, so I didn't even bother going to see him. Instead I decided that the best thing to do was to pray for God's healing. I asked God to heal me of the negative side effects of the vaccination upon my heart and body. God kindly answered my prayer, and the problem has completely gone.

These are just a few of the physical healings I've experienced in answer to prayer. I want to encourage you to pray and believe for God's healing for yourself. As I've already mentioned, Jesus Christ came to give us a full life, but that is often hampered by sickness or oppression we may be suffering with. When our lives are being destroyed, that is not God's will. He wants to bring healing into our lives, enabling us to live out a full and productive life for His kingdom purposes. Through this book you will learn how to pray prayers of faith that are powerful and effective, and see God move miraculously in your own life and those around you. Such prayer should be the norm for Christ's followers as He died for our sins *and* our sicknesses. Let's now look at a biblical example of someone who asked and received God's healing touch.

King Hezekiah's healing from a terminal illness

King Hezekiah was very sick and had been told by Isaiah the prophet that he was doing to die and needed to put his house in order. Hezekiah was broken upon hearing the news, and subsequently humbled himself, turning to God in prayer for healing:

> "In those days Hezekiah became ill and was at the point of death. The prophet Isaiah son of Amoz went to him and said, 'This is what the LORD says: Put your house in order, because you are going to die; you will not recover.' Hezekiah turned his face to the wall and prayed to the LORD, 'Remember, LORD, how I have walked before you faithfully and with wholehearted devotion and have done what is good in your eyes.' And Hezekiah wept bitterly.
> Before Isaiah had left the middle court, the word of the LORD came to him: 'Go back and tell Hezekiah, the ruler of my people, 'This is what the LORD, the God of your father David, says: I have heard your prayer and seen your tears; I will heal you. On the third day from now you will go up to the temple of the LORD. I will add fifteen years to your life. And I will deliver you and this city from the land of the king of Assyria. I will defend this city for my sake and for the sake of my servant David.'
> Then Isaiah said, 'Prepare a poultice of figs.' They did so and applied it to the boil, and he recovered.
> Hezekiah had asked Isaiah, 'What will be the sign that the LORD will heal me and that I will go up to the temple of the LORD on the third day from now?'

Isaiah answered, 'This is the LORD's sign to you that the LORD will do what he has promised: Shall the shadow go forward ten steps, or shall it go back ten steps?'
'It is a simple matter for the shadow to go forward ten steps,' said Hezekiah. 'Rather, have it go back ten steps.' Then the prophet Isaiah called on the LORD, and the LORD made the shadow go back the ten steps it had gone down on the stairway of Ahaz."
2 Kings 20:1-11

Hezekiah had been told by God that he needed to get his house in order as he was going to die. He had been given a terminal prognosis. However, the king decided he didn't want to accept that and believed that God could heal him. He wanted to live and was willing to humble himself before God, even with tears, and asked God to heal him.

There are two dramatic answers to prayer in this passage. Even after being told that God would heal him, Hezekiah's faith needed some encouragement and so he asked for a miraculous sign and God graciously granted that too. He made the shadow of the sun reverse back down the steps. As Jesus said, if you believe, you will receive whatever you ask for in prayer:

> "And I will do whatever you ask in my name, so that the Father may be glorified in the Son. You may ask me for anything in my name, and I will do it." John 14:13-14:

> "Ask and it will be given to you; seek and you will find; knock and the door will be opened to you. For everyone who asks receives; he who seeks finds; and to him who knocks, the door will be opened." Matthew 7:7-8

Matthew 7 reveal a prerequisite on our part: to ask, seek, and knock God's door (metaphorically speaking) for His attention. We need to seek God and ask Him for what we need. As we do, we will find the answers we're looking for. These promises are given to instil confidence when we pray.

It doesn't matter what the doctors may have told you, how grim the diagnosis may be, God is able and willing to answer the humble prayer of faith for healing. Only God can meet the deepest and most impossible of needs. The world is blessed with medical experts, but they can't always help us. God is our Healer and He alone can heal our broken hearts and bodies. He alone can deliver us from those things that destroy and oppress us.

Approaching God is possible because of Christ

Because of the shed blood of Christ, we can approach God. Christ's sacrifice on the cross not only defeated Satan and all his evil works, but also made forgiveness possible for us. Christ paid for all our sin and so we can be forgiven and reconciled with God our Father as we repent and turn to God in faith.

Forgiveness and healing is possible all because of Christ

That's why we pray in the name of Jesus Christ: it's all possible because of what He has done for us. We can therefore boldly approach God in prayer in Christ's name and implement Christ's victory.

All the blessings we receive from God are out of the kindness of God's grace and not because of our own merit. No one comes to the Father except through Him (John 14:6). Therefore when we pray in Christ's name, God will hear us and grant what we ask.

PART A

Prayer is therapeutic

Please don't make the mistake of thinking that God is too busy to pay attention to you. I've heard people say: *God has so many people on this planet to take care of with bigger problems than mine. I'm not going to trouble Him.* That might sound noble but it flies in the face of what God wants and teaches. He paid a great price for you to be able to approach Him and receive His blessings. Being the almighty God, He is more than able to give each of His children all the love and attention they need. God *wants* you to talk to Him about what's on your heart. He wants to hear. Jesus said, *when* you pray, not *if* you pray.

If you don't talk to God about what's really on your heart, how will your friendship with Him grow? How will you give Him the chance to show you what He can do if you're not asking Him for anything? We are invited to approach God with confidence:

> "Therefore, since we have a great high priest who has ascended into heaven, Jesus the Son of God, let us hold firmly to the faith we profess. For we do not have a high priest who is unable to empathize with our weaknesses, but we have one who has been tempted in every way, just as we are – yet he did not sin. Let us then approach God's throne of grace with confidence, so that we may receive mercy and find grace to help us in our time of need." Hebrews 4:14-16

Approaching God's throne of grace in prayer with confidence is a very important aspect of being a follower of Jesus Christ. Jesus repeated this invitation in Matthew 11: 28-30 (NLT):

"Come to me, all you who are weary and carry heavy burdens, and I will give you rest. Take my yoke upon you. Let me teach you, because I am humble and gentle at heart, and you will find rest for your souls. For my yoke is easy to bear, and the burden I give you is light."

I have found this to be so true. Many times I've come to God either feeling stressed or worried about things. However, when I pray and offload all my concerns to God, a transaction takes place: He in turn gives me His peace, guidance and reassurance. That's what Jesus is talking about here in Matthew 11. As you give God your burdens, He will minister to you by His Holy Spirit and through His Word. You will begin to hear God speaking to you and you will learn to discern His voice speaking words of comfort and instruction. Just spending time in God's presence talking to Him, asking for His help, will make a world of difference to how you will feel. And of course, He will answer your requests too.

I have found that coming to God, giving Him all my burdens, is by far the most effective way of dealing with problems. It also safeguards against worry and anxiety which does us no good. Prayer is therapeutic: God transforms how you feel. Best of all - it's all free.

Hebrews 4 teaches us that Jesus is our great High Priest, and as such, He stands in the gap between us and God the Father interceding for us. It's all because of what Jesus Christ has done for us that we can freely and boldly approach God in prayer. So turn to God. Just talk to Him and tell Him what's on your heart and what you need. It's therapeutic and He is waiting to hear from you. He loves it when you ask Him and trust Him to help you.

Specific prayers get specific answers

So don't be shy in asking God exactly what you need. You'll be blown away when He answers and that will do wonders for your faith levels and your understanding of God.

Freedom from pain

Contrary to what some people mistakenly think, God wants us to live lives free from lasting pain. Because of the world we live in, we are not immune from its unwelcome experience. However, as God's child, you can experience God's help and freedom in your life, whether the suffering is physical, emotional, mental, or spiritual. One man in the Bible who experienced freedom from pain was Jabez.

Jabez

The name, Jabez, literally means 'born in pain'. Yet he didn't want pain to be the trademark of his life. Read what he prayed for:

> "Jabez was more honourable than his brothers. His mother had named him Jabez, saying, 'I gave birth to him in pain.' Jabez cried out to the God of Israel, 'Oh, that you would bless me and enlarge my territory! Let your hand be with me, and keep me from harm so that I will be free from pain.' And God granted his request."
> 1 Chronicles 4:9-10

Can you imagine being given the name 'he who causes pain' by your mother? How must he have felt growing up with the reminder of what his mother went through to bring him into the world? We are told that Jabez was an honourable man, but he didn't want that legacy of pain to follow him all through his life. He wanted it's experience left in the past and wanted to live a life free from pain, and so he prays for blessing, protection from harm and a life free from pain. God answered his prayer and granted the request of this honourable man. Be inspired by Jabez and bring your requests to God in prayer. He loves to answer.

Jesus wants us to experience full lives that are free from pain (John 10:10). Jesus talked openly about the agenda and works of Satan. We often are afraid to even mention his name, but the Bible clearly teaches that he exists and many of his fallen angels (known as demons or unclean or evil spirits in the Bible), are busy trying to make people's lives miserable and full of pain and suffering. Jesus taught that the Devil wants to destroy us, but He wants to give us full lives.

Too often we blame God for what is actually Satan's handiwork

Living a full life and a life of pain at the same time are not meant to be cohabitees. I'm not saying that God wants to wrap us up in cotton so that we will never experience pain. Experiences happen: we lose our job, our loved ones, relationships break down and our hearts break. What I am saying is pain is not meant to be the defining characteristic in our lives. It's not meant to be permanent. God wants to set us free from pain and suffering whether it's physical, emotional, mental or spiritual. As John 10:10 teaches, Jesus Christ came to give us an abundant life, not one characterised by pain, death and destruction. He came to destroy the works of the Devil (1 John 3:8).

I remember a story that a friend of mine shared with me of how God helped a friend of hers who had gone through a very difficult time personally, but how God had met her and healed her of her emotional pain and heartbreak. This is what she shared:

When our two daughters were about 2 and 4 years old, we met another mom and her two daughters of same ages at a playground near our home. We all became fast friends and spent a lot of time together. Our oldest two started school together, and the younger ones continued having play dates. Our husbands also became friends and consequently our families visited each other often. One morning my friend, June, phoned me unexpectedly to tell me they would not be coming for dinner as planned. When I asked why not, she burst into tears and told me that her husband had left her and wouldn't be coming back. It was utter shock for both of us. Neither of us had any inclination this would happen. As we cried many, many tears together, I felt like my own heart would break because of the pain. I knew that I could not do anything but pray for her. She was not a Christian and had no desire to hear about God, but we prayed for her like we have never prayed for anyone before... a lot! I also gave her a Bible and wrote the verse from Jeremiah 29:11 in it: "for I know the plans I have for you" declares the LORD, "plans to prosper you and not to harm you, plans to give you hope and a future."

After a while my husband was called to pastor a church in a different city and Jane also moved to be closer to her parents. We kept in touch, but very sporadically. That was before Facebook. After about a year June and her daughters came to our city to visit us. June told me with tears in her eyes that when I gave her the Bible, she looked at it but couldn't understand it. The verse didn't make any sense to her, etc. She put it away. Then after she moved, she met someone who invited her to their church and she actually went and liked it (I had invited her to mine as well when we lived in the same place, but she wasn't that interested). Long story short, she had become a Christian, loved her church, read her Bible all the time, and had just been asked to start a ministry to single parents. She told me that her Bible, our friendship, that Jeremiah scripture, were a huge part of her testimony that she had shared many times since becoming a Christian. I was blown away that those prayers and tears from more than a year ago had been a part of where she was now.

God can turn those unexpected situations around in our lives, heal our pain and bring us hope and a future. That's God's handiwork. When something traumatic happens that you don't expect, not only do you have to deal with the pain of it all, but there are also numerous practical needs you are suddenly faced with. It can feel so overwhelming. You see your life going in one direction, and before you know it, things have taken a completely unexpected turn. At times like this, the best thing we can do is turn to God in prayer and ask for His help and guidance.

I've experienced this myself when my first marriage broke down. I didn't see it coming and as a church pastor, I never thought it would happen to me. But it did. God revealed things to me that had been going on, which I was completely unaware of, and brought me guidance, comfort and strength through a very painful season. I don't think I've ever prayed and sought God so much as I did during that period of my life. I needed God, I needed to know His will and guidance, and His practical provision too. I hadn't needed an income as a church planter as my husband had provided and so I was suddenly faced with having to find a new source of income too, not just for me but also for the church. God was so faithful and guided and provided step by step. I found a paid part time job, got a new home for myself and the church, and God comforted and healed my confused and broken heart. Most people around me did not understand what was really going on (I didn't completely understand it myself until later), but I know that my loving Heavenly Father dramatically moved in my life to rescue His vulnerable child who loved Him from a harmful situation. I am so grateful to God for His faithfulness through one of the most painful times in my life. God is always faithful when we turn to Him in prayer.

> *Things may happen you may not have foreseen, but God has foreseen it all, and He faithfully works to provide for you.*

In those moments, God is still in control. Nothing surprises God and He can heal your broken heart and guide you to a place of hope and blessing despite the ordeal. The best thing you can do is pray and lean on God for His help and provision. He will comfort and heal your heart and provide for you practically too. God is able to bring you through the painful seasons of life into great victory. God can take what the enemy meant for harm and bring great good out of it. If you have been living with pain for a long time, I will show you through this book how to be set free. Please keep reading.

God can work all things together for good through prayer

Although, as Jesus explained, the Devil tries to bring destructive experiences into our lives, God can dramatically turn things around for good for us. God can lead us into victory as we trust Him, enabling us to plunder the enemy's camp. Romans 8:28 (ESV) makes a wonderful promise:

> "And we know that for those who love God all things work together for good, for those who are calling according to his purpose."

No matter what is thrown at you, God can take that and work it together for good in our lives. It might be hard to imagine at the time, but God is so great and so powerful (far more powerful than the defeated Devil), and as you pray, God will take what the enemy meant for harm and turn it around, bringing great good into your life in a way that it will not only benefit you, but will enable you to help others through their trials too.

Draw near to God in prayer and read His Word through the painful times, and you will experience God speaking to you, bringing much-needed comfort and strength, healing and guidance. God is on your side, and He will provide for you as you pray. In June's story, her friend's prayers were instrumental in June finding God and a new hope and future for her life. Prayer dramatically changed things for the better for June as I too have found. Such is the power of prayer.

God can do far more than you can imagine

God moves in response to our prayers. If we don't ask, we don't receive. It's a simple principle, which is the same in all areas of life. If you don't ask for that new job, you won't get it. If you don't ask for a meal in a restaurant, you'll go hungry. If your friend doesn't ask for help, they won't receive it. We often don't have something simply because we have not asked God. James 4:3 talks about this:

> You do not have because you do not ask God. When you ask, you do not receive, because you ask with wrong motives, that you may spend what you get on your pleasures.

We can ask God for what we need and trust Him to answer because he loves us. Proverbs 3:5-6 promise that:

"Trust in the LORD with all your heart and lean not on our own understanding; in all your ways submit to him, and he will make your paths straight."

I've held on to that promise many times over the years, especially when I had no idea what direction my life was going in. There have been quite a few of those moments. What I have found is that when we surrender to God, trust Him with all our heart, and stop trying to figure things out on our own, He will guide us.

God's ways and timing is different to ours. He may not work according to your time frame or way that you expect, because His timing and ways are higher and perfect. Ours aren't. It will take a lot of trust and sometimes patience, but waiting for God is so worth it. God's ways are better than our own. God's plans for your life are far greater than anything you can dream up for yourself. Listen to what Paul the apostle wrote in Ephesians 3:14-20 (NLT):

> When I think of all this, I fall to my knees and pray to the Father, the Creator of everything in heaven and on earth. I pray that from his glorious, unlimited resources he will empower you with inner strength through his Spirit. Then Christ will make his home in your heart as you trust in him. Your roots will grow down into God's love and keep you strong. And may you have the power to understand, as all God's people should, how wide, how long, how high, and how deep his love is. May you experience the love of Christ, though it is too great to understand fully. Then you will be made complete with all the fullness of life and power that comes from God. **Now all glory to God, who is able, through his mighty power at work within us, to accomplish infinitely more than we might ask or think**. (author's emphasis)

Because of how much God loves you, God is able to accomplish infinitely more than you can even ask or think through your prayers. I have walked with God for thirty-five years and I can confirm that God works in the most amazing ways you cannot even imagine. Life with God can be an adventure if you're willing to trust Him with all your heart and follow Him wherever He leads. God has a wonderful plan for your life that's beyond your imagination, better than anything you could dream up for yourself. You just need to trust Him with all your heart and follow Him.

As we have seen, there are many benefits to prayer. God wants to bring hope, healing, guidance, and miraculous provision through the challenging seasons of life. Prayer is powerful and as you draw near to God, not only will you see Him answer your prayers, but you will also grow in your knowledge of Him, and His power and love. God is so very good.

Prayer

Father God, thank you for your love for me and for the abundant life You want to bless me with. Let your hand be with me and keep me from harm. Bless me and my loved ones and guide me into your purposes for my life. Please help me understand how much you love me and how powerful prayer is. In the name of Jesus Christ

PART A

Questions for further study

1. After reading this chapter, what would you say are some benefits of prayer?

2. Have you experienced an answer to prayer in your own life?

3. Read Mark 1:35. What do we learn about Jesus in this verse? Why do you think Jesus prayed?

4. Read Luke 11:5-10. What does Jesus teach about prayer in these verses? What are we encouraged to do? What does Jesus promise?

5. In 1 Samuel 1:1-20, what did Hannah pray for? How did God answer her prayer?

6. What did Hannah do according to 1 Samuel 1:24-28?

7. How else did God bless Hannah according to 1 Samuel 2:18-21? What kind of man did Samuel become?

Chapter 2

Praying in the Holy Spirit

"When Apollos was at Corinth, Paul took the road through the interior and arrived at Ephesus. There he found some disciples and asked them, 'Did you receive the Holy Spirit when you believed?' They answered, 'No, we have not even heard that there is a Holy Spirit.' So Paul asked, 'Then what baptism did you receive?' 'John's baptism', they replied. Paul said, 'John's baptism was a baptism of repentance. He told the people to believe in the one coming after him, that is, in Jesus.' On hearing this, they were baptised in the name of the Lord Jesus. When Paul placed his hands on them, the Holy Spirit came on them, and they spoke in tongues and prophesied. There were about twelve men in all." Acts 19:1-7

Born of water and the Holy Spirit

The Holy Spirit, third Person of the Trinity of God (Matthew 28:19), accomplishes a number of very important roles for believers. Firstly, the Holy Spirit works in our salvation, bringing about our new birth:

"Truly, truly, I say to you, unless one is born of water and the Spirit, he cannot enter the kingdom of God. That which is born of the flesh is flesh, and that which is born of the Spirit is spirit." John 3:5-6 (ESV)

"He saved us through the washing of rebirth and renewal by the Holy Spirit, whom he poured on us generously through Jesus Christ our Saviour, so that, having been justified by his grace, we might become heirs having the hope of eternal life." Titus 3:5-7

The Bible teaches we need to be born of the Holy Spirit and water to see the kingdom of God. Repenting of our sins and putting our faith in Christ to forgive and save us initiates this process. God the Holy Spirit comes and renews us spiritually, making us born again and alive in Christ. Being baptised in water symbolises how we are washed from our sins and made new (Acts 22:16). God by His Holy Spirit provides us with many additional blessings.

God makes His home in our lives by His Spirit

Speaking about His Holy Spirit in John 14:15-17 and 23 (ESV), Jesus said:

"And I will ask the Father, and he will give you another Helper to be with you forever, even the Spirit of truth, whom the world cannot receive, because it neither sees him nor knows him. You know him, for he dwells with you and will be in you…
Jesus answered him, 'If anyone loves me, he will keep my word, and my Father will love him, and we will come to him and make our home with him.'"

When God comes and makes His home in our lives through the presence of His Holy Spirit, God lives in us 24/7. We have His presence continually with us, and He guides, strengthens, comforts, and encourages us through life. God promises to always be with us and to never leave us. He is your Helper through the many challenges of life and your closest Friend. No matter what you go through, with God in your life, you are never alone and never abandoned. God loves you and as Romans 8:31 says, if God is for us, who can be against us? God always wants to lead you into victory. There is no greater blessing than God making His home in our lives.

In addition to all this, God, by His Holy Spirit, also equips and empowers us to live the full life Jesus promised and to fulfil His kingdom purpose in our lives.

The baptism of the Holy Spirit

The baptism of the Holy Spirit is a special filling and endowment from God available to all believers in Christ, providing the power and spiritual gifts (abilities) we need to fulfil God's kingdom purposes.

In our opening verses of Acts 19, Paul asked the believers whether they had received the Holy Spirit when they first believed. The only baptism they had received was a water baptism. They hadn't even heard there was a Holy Spirit and so Paul proceeded to pray over them, that they may be baptised with the Holy Spirit. The Spirit came upon them, and they started speaking in tongues and prophesying.

The baptism of the Holy Spirit empowers and equips us to do God's kingdom work.

If you have decided to follow God, ask Him to baptise you with His Holy Spirit. God wants to endow you through His Holy Spirit with spiritual gifts to enable you to fulfil your God-given purpose in life and bless others. This was Peter's experience. After God poured out His Holy Spirit upon the disciples, Peter developed a powerful preaching and leadership ministry, which led many to faith in Christ:

> "'In the last days, God says, I will pour out my Spirit on all people. Your sons and daughters will prophesy, your young men will see visions, your old men will dream dreams. Even on my servants, both men and women, I will pour out my Spirit in those days, and they will prophesy…
> Repent and be baptised, every one of you, in the name of Jesus Christ for the forgiveness of your sins. And you will receive the gift of the Holy Spirit. The promise is for you and your children and for all who are far off – for all whom the Lord our God will call.'
> Those who accepted his message were baptised, and about three thousand were added to their number that day." Acts 2:17 to 18, 38 to 39, and 41.

God gives His Holy Spirit freely through His grace and kindness as Peter learned in Acts 10:44-48 when preaching to Gentiles:

> "While Peter was still speaking these words, the Holy Spirit came on all who heard the message. The circumcised believers who had come with Peter were astonished that the gift of the Holy Spirit had been poured out even on Gentiles. For they heard them speaking in tongues and praising God. Then Peter said, 'Surely no one can stand in the way of their being baptized with water. They have received the Holy Spirit just as we have. So he ordered that they be baptised in the name of the Jesus Christ."

No one can earn this blessing of the baptism of the Holy Spirit. As with everything we have in Christ, God's

Spirit is freely poured out through God's grace. Peter came to understand this as he recounted what happened in the following chapter to the church in Jerusalem:

> "As I began to speak, the Holy Spirit came on them as he had come on us at the beginning. Then I remembered what the Lord had said, 'John baptised with water, but you will be baptised with the Holy Spirit.'" Acts 11:15-16

As Peter learned, the gift of the baptism of the Holy Spirit is for everyone whom God calls. If you sincerely desire more of God and want to fulfil His purpose in your life, ask God to fill you with His Holy Spirit. Receiving the filling of the Holy Spirit is something that all believers can and should ask God for. God wants to pour His Spirit into your life for without Him, we are walking in our own strength, and that won't get us very far. God by His Holy Spirit enables us to live a victorious life and fulfil God's plan for our lives.

Equipped with spiritual gifts

When God fills us with His Holy Spirit, the Holy Spirit gives us spiritual gifts, which equip, empower and motivate believers to serve God. Some gifts appear more practical such as teaching, giving, administration, or service, while others appear supernatural such as speaking in tongues, prophecy, miraculous powers, interpretation of tongues, and gifts of healing. Whatever the gift, they are all effective and useful in God's kingdom and provided by God the Holy Spirit.

There are several passages in the Bible that talk about spiritual gifts and their purpose, which are all still available today to those who follow Christ:

> "For just as each of us has one body with many members, and these members do not all have the same function,

so in Christ we, though many, form one body, and each member belongs to all the others. We have different gifts, according to the grace given to each of us. If your gift is **prophesying**, then prophesy in accordance with your faith; if it is **serving**, then serve; if it is **teaching,** then teach; if it is to **encourage**, then give encouragement; if it is **giving**, then give generously; if it is to **lead**, do it diligently; if it so to **show mercy**, do it cheerfully." Romans 12:4-8 (author's emphasis)

"Now you are the body of Christ, and each of you is a part of it. And God has placed in the church first of all **apostles**, second **prophets**, third **teachers**, then **miracles**, then **gifts of healing**, of helping, of guidance, and of different kinds of tongues. Are all apostles? Are all prophets? Are all teachers? Do all work miracles? Do all have gifts of healing? Do all speak in tongues? Do all interpret? Now eagerly desire the greater gifts." 1 Corinthians 12:27-31 (author's emphasis)

"There are different kinds of gifts, but the same Spirit distributes them. There are different kinds of service, but the same Lord. There are different kinds of working, but in all of them and in everyone it is the same God at work. Now to each one the manifestation of the Spirit is given for the common good. To one there is given through the Spirit a message of **wisdom**, to another a **message of knowledge** by means of the same Spirit, to another **faith** by the same Spirit, to another **gifts of healing** by that one Spirit, to another **miraculous powers**, to another **prophecy**, to another **distinguishing between spirits**, to another **speaking in different kinds of tongues**, and to still others the **interpretation of tongues**. All these are the work of the one and same Spirit, and he distributes them to each one, just as he determines." 1 Corinthians 12:4-11 (author's emphasis)

The Holy Spirit gives spiritual gifts to those who believe in God through Christ, and God's gifts play an important role in understanding what our God-given purpose is, including the role we can play in our local church. They're not given to boost our egos, but to build up and encourage us and others around us. They're meant to be used to be a blessing not only in our own lives but also to help and support others:

> "Each of you should use whatever gift you have received to serve others, as faithful stewards of God's grace in its various forms. If anyone speaks, they should do so as one who speaks the very words of God. If anyone serves, they should do so with the strength God provides, so that in all things God may be praised through Jesus Christ. To him be the glory and the power for ever and ever. Amen." 1 Peter 4:10-11

Understanding and operating in your spiritual gifts are essential for every believer. They are not an optional add-on. Where members of a church are encouraged to discover and operate in their gifts, you will find members busy at work. The pastor is not meant to do all the work. Their role is to equip the believers to fulfil God's purpose. The gifts point to how God has equipped and gifted you to bless others around you. Not only are they a great blessing to others, but they can bring much joy and satisfaction into your own life as you see God using you as an instrument for His kingdom purposes.

I will spend some time now on the gift of speaking in tongues as the topic of this book is prayer, which is a main context in which tongues is used.

Speaking in tongues

After Jesus had risen from the dead but before He ascended back into heaven, He told His disciples that He was going to send the Holy Spirit to give them power to enable them to be witnesses of the Gospel message (Acts 1:8). The believers didn't have to wait long before God poured out His Holy Spirit upon the believers just as Jesus had promised:

> "Suddenly a sound like the blowing of a violent wind came from heaven and filled the whole house where they were sitting. They saw what seemed to be tongues of fire that separated and came to rest on each of them. All of them were filled with the Holy Spirit and began to speak in other tongues as the Spirit enabled them." Acts 2:2-4

After the disciples received the Holy Spirit, they became emboldened to preach the gospel message of salvation, and miracles and healings followed. They were also given the gift of speaking in tongues, praying to and worshipping God in a different language. We've read a number of passages where believers were given the gift of speaking in tongues following Holy Spirit baptism. It might seem strange at first to see someone speaking in a different language that they haven't previously learned, but essentially what is happening is God's Holy Spirit is praying and speaking through you. It is a wonderful privilege and is available to followers of Christ today, not just the first century Christians:

> "He [Jesus] said to them, 'Go into all the world and preach the gospel to all creation. Whoever believes and is baptised will be saved, but whoever does not believe will be condemned. And these signs will accompany those who believe: In my name they will drive out demons; they will speak in new tongues; they will pick up snakes

with their hands; and when they drink deadly poison, it will not hurt them at all; they will place their hands on sick people, and they will get well." Mark 16:15-18

The purposes of speaking in tongues

The gift of speaking in tongues has several purposes. Firstly, it's a gift of prayer where the Holy Spirit is praying and interceding through you:

> "And **pray in the Spirit** on all occasions with all kinds of prayers and requests. With this in mind, be alert and always keep on praying for all the Lord's people." Ephesians 6:18 (author's emphasis)

What does it mean to pray in the Spirit? Well, there are two aspects to this. Firstly, you can ask God at the start of your prayer time to lead you by His Holy Spirit and show you who and what to pray for. God can bring people or situations to mind that need your prayers. Prayer should be a two-way experience, not just us talking to God. I've had my best ideas from being quiet before God in prayer, allowing Him to guide my thoughts, bringing ideas and Scriptures to mind, showing me the best way forward.

A second aspect of praying in the Spirit is to pray using the gift of tongues. This is when you are given the ability by the Holy Spirit to pray in a different language. When God prays through you by His Holy Spirit using this gift, you can be assured that those prayers are most powerful and effective, perfectly in line with God's will. After all, the Holy Spirit is doing the praying! That's why the Bible encourages us to pray in the Holy Spirit. It's a wonderful blessing and privilege to have God the Holy Spirit intercede through us using the gift of tongues. He understands what is needed and knows exactly how to pray most effectively to bring down God's power to earth.

Some may only have a word or two when they first start using this gift; others may have more. If you don't yet have the gift and desire it, ask God to bless you with it. To start, take a step of faith and open your mouth and talk in your native language. Just say something to get your mouth moving. It's easier to direct a moving car than a stationary one. Don't let the fear of looking foolish or shyness hold you back. It might be your native language to begin with, but foreign words will follow. As you practice the gift, it will develop and increase as with any ability. If you are faithful in using and developing the gift, you may find that God gives you additional prayer languages over time.

Whenever I pray in tongues, I often feel led by the Holy Spirit to do so. But I don't always have to wait for His prompting; I can pray in tongues anytime I desire as I'm in complete control of the gift. I often know the subject I'm praying about, even though I don't understand the words. I can also pray with my mind in my own native language at the same time. Some people will also have the gift of interpretation of speaking in tongues, which provides a translation of the prayer tongue and so they will know exactly what they are praying.

Sometimes God will use the gift in us to engage in spiritual warfare prayer. Ephesians 6 explains how we are in a spiritual battle against evil, and praying in tongues is a weapon God has given us to overcome evil.

> *Praying in tongues in the Holy Spirit is a weapon God has given us to overcome evil*

I have found praying in tongues to be important when praying and interceding for others who are in desperate places. When I'm not sure how to pray for someone, I pray in tongues. Often when I pray for healing or deliverance for someone, I will use this gift, allowing God the Holy Spirit to intercede. After all, when we pray for these kinds of needs, we are confronting forces of evil in the heavenly realms. It's a spiritual battle and it's more effective to allow God the Holy Spirit to engage in battle through you by using this gift. I find that problems are dealt with much quicker and more effectively when I pray in tongues led by the Holy Spirit.

Engaging in spiritual warfare through tongues will sometimes feel authoritative. I remember one time when a relative had told me that her fiancé's father was dying. He was most upset because he wouldn't be able to reach his father in time to say goodbye before he passed away as he lived overseas. A few days after hearing that news, I was pulling up to park my car when out of the blue, I suddenly felt the Holy Spirit move me to pray for this situation. I found myself sat in my car praying authoritatively in tongues (as well as my native language), that the father wouldn't yet die before his son had the chance to see him and say goodbye. I was quite surprised as I hadn't been thinking of doing that at that moment, but I knew this was God's prompting, waging war by His Holy Spirit in the heavenly realms against the wicked deeds of the evil one.

Some time later, the fiancé told me how his father hadn't died when was expected and how he'd had the chance to say goodbye. This is a good example of being led by the Holy Spirit to intercede and pray for someone using the gift of tongues, doing warfare by the Holy Spirit, overcoming the evil works of the enemy. I encourage you to ask God to give you this gift as it really is powerful and effective.

In addition to using the gift for prayer is using the gift to worship God, whether through spoken words or singing in tongues. It's a wonderful experience to be led by the Holy Spirit to sing in worship using the gift of tongues. You may see this happen in churches, but it can also be done in private prayer. It always sounds beautiful when it happens. God is not looking for fine voices but sincere hearts of worship.

Prophecy is yet another purpose of the gift when accompanied by an interpretation. God gives some people a gift of interpretation of tongues, which is essentially a prophetic use of the gift and often takes place in group settings. There is a gift of prophecy itself but the gift of interpretation can also be used for the same purpose. Someone may feel led to publicly speak out in faith and give a message in tongues, and then someone else will provide the interpretation. Prophecy is used to bring messages of encouragement or guidance from God for the people listening:

> "Pursue love, and earnestly desire the spiritual gifts, especially that you may prophesy. For one who speaks in a tongue speaks not to men but to God for no one understands him, but he utters mysteries in the Spirit. On the other hand, the one who prophesies speaks to people for their upbuilding and encouragement and consolation. The one who speaks in a tongue builds up himself, but the one who prophesies builds up the church. Now I want you all to speak in tongues, but even more to prophesy. The one who prophesies in greater than the one who speaks in tongues, unless someone interprets, so that the church may be built up." 1 Corinthians 14:1-5.

All of the gifts of the Holy Spirit are a blessing, but the more people a spiritual gift can help, the greater the gift, and 1 Corinthians 12:31 encourages us to seek God for them.

PART A

Exercise the gifts in love

One very important factor to remember as we seek to operate in God's spiritual gifts is found in 1 Corinthians 13:1-3:

> "If I speak in the tongues of men or of angels, but do not have love, I am only a resounding gong or a clanging cymbal. If I have the gift of prophecy and can fathom all mysteries and knowledge, and if I have a faith that can move mountains, but do not have love, I am nothing. If I give all I possess to the poor and give over my body to hardship that I may boast, but do not have love, I gain nothing."

No matter what spiritual gifts we may operate in, or how generous or sacrificial we are, unless we operate in love, we are nothing and gain nothing. Love is paramount to God for God is love (1 John 4:16) and He calls us to love our neighbour. In fact, the Bible teaches that if we do not love others, we don't really know God (1 John 4:8) no matter what we profess. Loving others is more important to God than exercising the gifts, and the minute we stop using our gifts out of love and humility, we step outside of God's will. Loving others must always be a priority when using our gifts and we must never use our gifts out of pride, selfish ambition or boasting:

> "Love is patient, love is kind. It does not envy, it does not boast, it is not proud. It does not dishonour others, it is not self-seeking, it is not easily angered, it keeps no record of wrongs. Love does not delight in evil but rejoices with the truth. It always protects, always trusts, always hopes, always perseveres. Love never fails." 1 Corinthians 13: 4 to 8

Don't make the mistake of placing greater importance on using your gifts than on loving your brother and sister in Christ. God gives His gifts for a reason, to be a sincere blessing and encouragement to others in Christ's Church as well as to encourage ourselves. However, the moment we promote ourselves at the expense of loving our brother and sister in Christ, we miss the whole point and expose a lack of maturity in God. Walking in love is greater and how we relate to and treat one another will reveal our true character and maturity. God will promote you when He knows you're ready and not before.

The gift of tongues then can be used for different purposes: prayer, worship and prophecy. If you don't have the gift of tongues, you have no need to be disheartened. There are many other gifts. God decides what gifts to give to whom according to His purpose is for your life. Perhaps God has a greater gift for you. More people should seek after the gifts of faith, evangelism, prophecy, healing and miraculous powers. Imagine how those gifts could bless people and heal our broken world? I am inspired by healing evangelist Robby Dawkins. He ministers all over the world and has gone into some of the most dangerous countries, including front lines of war, to pray for the sick and bring the message of the gospel of Christ, which has the power to heal families, communities and nations. He is using his spiritual gifts of healing, teaching, service and evangelism to bless and help countless people. If you don't know what your spiritual gifts are, there are many books on the subject. I recommend using a spiritual gifts assessment which can be very helpful.[1]

---

[1] I find the spiritual gifts assessment by C. Peter Wagner very good.

PART A

A word for church leaders

Some church leaders are afraid of teaching on the subject of spiritual gifts for fear of excesses. This fear withholds great blessing from churches and its members and is disobedient to what the Bible teaches about the great blessing and encouragement spiritual gifts can be. When church members know what their spiritual gifts are and are given the opportunity to exercise them, the Church grows and becomes more productive and effective. People start stepping up because they become motivated and excited to use their gifts and serve God. However, when church members are not taught about the gifts and this blessing is withheld, they're not only robbing their members of their purpose, but also their church and community from great blessing and assistance. It's no wonder people aren't then motivated to serve.

Through helping church members discover and operate in their gifts, I have seen homeless, food poverty, sick, addiction and prison ministries develop because members felt inspired and motivated to make a difference in their local community. If your church members are not serving much, encourage them to find out what their gifts are and provide opportunities for them to use them. You will see the positive difference it makes to your church.

Spiritual gifts are powerful and effective in driving forward the Great Commission that Jesus entrusted to us:

> "Then Jesus came to them and said, 'All authority in heaven and on earth has been given to me. Therefore go and make disciples of all nations, baptising them in the name of the Father and of the Son and of the Holy Spirit, and teaching them to obey everything I have commanded you. And surely I am with you always, to the very end of the age.'" Matthew 28:18-20

If any member begins to operate a spiritual gift excessively, having a policy in place on how and when the gifts can and cannot be used will help address it. For example, prophetic messages can only be given publicly by those who are trusted with the gift, or not having more than two or three prophetic messages in any given service, or not allowing the gifts to be used during communion when people desire quietness before God. Don't rob your church and your local community of the great blessing of exercising the gifts of the Holy Spirit.

Utilise the armour of God

God wants you to walk in victory in your life. Whilst there is much good going on in the world, media feeds prove that there is also evil at work. The Bible teaches that we are in a battle with evil powers, but the good news is we are not alone nor without mighty defence to overcome.

In addition to the spiritual gifts that God blesses us with, God has also provided us with armour, powerful spiritual weapons that we can use to stand, fight and overcome all powers of the evil one as Ephesians 6:10-18 explains:

> "Finally, be strong in the Lord and in his mighty power. Put on the full armour of God, so that you can take your stand against the Devil's schemes. For our struggle is not against flesh and blood, but against the rulers, against the authorities, against the powers of this dark world and against the spiritual forces of evil in the heavenly realms. Therefore put on the full armour of God, so that when the day of evil comes, you may be able to stand your ground, and after you have done everything, so stand. Stand firm then, with the **belt of truth** buckled around your waist, with the **breastplate of righteousness** in place, and with your feet **fitted with the readiness** that comes from the

gospel of peace. In addition to all this, take up the **shield of faith**, with which you can extinguish all the flaming arrows of the evil one. Take the **helmet of salvation** and the **sword of the Spirit, which is the word of God**.
And **pray in the Spirit on all occasions with all kinds of prayers and requests**. With this in mind, be alert and always keep on praying for all the Lord's people." (author's emphasis)

This important passage teaches us how to find victory in the daily battles we find ourselves in. It's crucially important that we use the various pieces of the armour of God to stand firm in our faith and resist and overcome the attacks of the evil one. In addition to praying in the Holy Spirit, other weapons at our disposal include the powerful and enduring Word of God (the Bible), and faith which, when exercised, acts like a shield against those fiery arrows of the evil one. Walking in truth and righteousness, and being confident of one's salvation, also serve to protect us. These weapons are not meant to be prayed on like some kind of magic protection. Rather they are meant to be applied and exercised in every personal battle we face.

The armour of God is meant to be applied and exercised

God's armour is powerful and as we use what God has given us, we will see victory and demolish the work of the enemy:

"For though we live in the world, we do not wage war as the world does. The weapons we fight with are not the weapons of the world. On the contrary, **they have divine power to demolish strongholds**." 2 Corinthians 10:3-4 (author's emphasis)

God's weapons are powerful and when used, can destroy and defeat every scheme and stronghold of the evil one. You have no reason to fear or live in defeat. When we walk in faith, truth, righteousness, confidence of salvation, by the Word of God, praying in the Holy Spirit, we are employing the powerful weapons God has given us to overcome every attack of the enemy:

> "'No weapon that is formed against you will succeed; And every tongue that rises against you in judgment you will condemn. This [peace, righteousness, security, and triumph over opposition] is the heritage of the servants of the LORD, And this is their vindication from Me,' says the LORD." Isaiah 54:17 (Amp)

In Christ, we can walk in victory, so utilise the armour that God has provided and pray in the Holy Spirit, and you will overcome every battle you face as I experienced recently.

Healing from lump in my breast

A short while ago whilst writing this book, God showed me through dreams that I was going to come under spiritual attack. Sure enough, a few weeks later, I woke up one morning with a painful lump in my right breast. It felt about one and half inches in diameter, and it was painful, tender and sore. It felt inflamed and of course, I was concerned.

Whenever faced with a health problem, we always have choices to make. For me in this occasion, I felt my choice was either turn to the doctors and go down the medical route, or trust God alone to heal. God can (and does) use doctors whom He has wonderfully gifted, but on this occasion, I felt that if I did that, I would not be walking in faith, trusting God to heal me, but the opposite. Medical specialists, as brilliant and skilled as they are, are not always able to solve all our physical problems. Plus there are very long waiting lists to see specialists here in the UK, so obtaining the medical treatment we need is not always easy. Whenever I thought about going down the medical route, if felt like I would be putting my trust in people rather than God, essentially taking a step of "non-faith".[2] The Bible teaches that God is our Healer, and so I decided I would look to God alone for the healing I needed and believe He could do a far better and quicker job too. My plan was to put on the belt of truth and take up the sword of the Spirit and immerse my heart and mind in the promises of God for healing, which I knew would strengthen my shield of faith which I needed, plus at the same time, earnestly seek God in prayer and pray in the Holy Spirit.

God touched my heart through the verses of Matthew 9:28-30 and used those few verses to minister to my heart:

> "When he had gone indoors, the blind men came to him, and he asked them, 'Do you believe that I am able to do this?' 'Yes, Lord.' they replied. Then he touched their eyes and said, 'According to your faith will it be done to you'; and their sight was restored."

For a whole week, by His Holy Spirit, God spoke to me and encouraged me through these words, highlighting a different phrase each day. On the first day God asked me: *Do you believe I am able to do this?* I meditated on that and felt my faith being challenged and encouraged. Did I believe that God was able? I thought about that. I decided, yes Lord, I believe you are able.

The next day, He spoke to me: *According to your faith will it be done to you*. God was highlighting how it would be by faith that I would be healed.

---

[2] A word I use to mean the opposite of walking by faith.

HOW TO PRAY FOR HEALING, FREEDOM AND DELIVERANCE

Faith is invisible but its reality is lived out visibly.

My faith mattered and I needed to live like I believed. I understood that it is by faith that we receive miraculous answers from God and my healing would come by faith.

The day after that, God highlighted to me: *When He had gone indoors, the blind men came to Him.* These men pursued Jesus for healing. They didn't sit on the sidelines and say to themselves, 'If it's God's will, Jesus will heal us.' The previous verses show how they had been calling out to Jesus, garnering His attention and asking for His mercy on them. They didn't stop there, for they had the audacity to follow Jesus into the house to pursue Him for their healing. They weren't concerned about interrupting Him, or whether He had more important cases to address first. They followed Jesus by faith and as a result, they received their healing. I needed to do the same. So I sought God in prayer and asked Him to heal me completely. In the name of Jesus Christ, I also rebuked every scheme and unclean spirit of the enemy against me. I prayed God would deliver me from evil and for God's kingdom to come and His will to be done in my life. And I prayed in tongues.

The following day, the Lord spoke to me through: *Then he touched their eyes.* Jesus granted their request. He touched them and their eyes were opened. Jesus followed through and performed the healing miracle they were hoping for. God spoke to my heart: He *will* perform the healing I needed. He *will* touch my body and heal me.

For that whole week, God ministered to me through those few years and by the end of it, the lump had completely disappeared and I was healed. The alternative would have been spending many months pursuing appointments and treatment for an outcome that would have been nowhere as complete as the healing God gave. Just as their sight was restored, so was my breast. Just by standing on these few verses and allowing God to minister to me through them, using the weapons of God's armour, building and strengthening my faith, God led me into complete healing. The lump had gone: no pain, no tenderness, no discomfort at all. I am so very grateful to God. The enemy tried to defeat and destroy me, but by taking up the sword of the Spirit, my shield of faith, and the belt of truth, God led me into complete victory over the enemy's attack. God can do the same for you.

Just as Jesus asked the two blind men, *"Do you believe I am able to do this?"* so He asks you today. Whatever need you are facing, as you put all your hope and trust in Him and His Word, He will answer you. Take up the armour of God and spend time meditating on God's promises, which will strengthen and build your faith. Use your shield of faith and put on the belt of truth. Ask God to lead your prayers by His Holy Spirit and God will lead you into victory:

> "Yet in all these things we are more than conquerors and gain an overwhelming victory through Him who loved us [so much that He died for us]." Romans 8:37 (Amp)

God's spiritual gifts and armour have been given to us to use and fulfil God's kingdom purposes in our lives. We are not meant to live defeated lives but can walk in victory as we use what God has given us to overcome every trial. As believers, we are filled with God's Holy Spirit and have God's presence and power with us 24/7. Discover the power of praying in the Holy Spirit and ask God to speak to you and guide you. Walking with God is an adventure as you trust and follow His guidance in your life.

Questions for further study

1. In your own words, what are some of the blessings of God dwelling in our lives?

2. Why do you think it's important to be baptised with God's Holy Spirit?

3. Have you tried praying in the Holy Spirit, whether asking God to lead you or praying in tongues?

4. From what you have learned, why does God give us gifts through the Holy Spirit? Do you know what gift(s) God has given you? If not, why not do a spiritual gifts assessment to find out?

5. Have you ever used God's armour when faced with a spiritual battle? If yes, please share that example.

6. Which piece of the armour do you think you need to use more?

7. Have you asked God to fill you with His Holy Spirit yet? If not, why not pray for that today? Pray the following prayer:

Lord God, I thank you that you give us your Holy Spirit to be with me and to be my Helper. God, please fill and baptise me with your Holy Spirit. Please bless me with your spiritual gifts so I can serve you and fulfil your purpose in my life. Help me to grow in you and know your guidance and direction for my life. In the name of Jesus Christ, amen.

Chapter 3

God speaks by His Holy Spirit

> "Now an angel of the Lord said to Philip, 'Go south to the road – the desert road – that goes down from Jerusalem to Gaza.'" Acts 8:26

In the previous chapter, we looked at how God gives spiritual gifts to equip us for His kingdom work here on earth, and armour to enable us to overcome the schemes and wiles of the Devil. We've also looked at what praying in the Holy Spirit means and the role of speaking in tongues in prayer. In addition to these great blessings, God wants to speak *to us* by His Spirit. Prayer should be two-way communication and God wants to provide guidance and encouragement we need in response to our prayers. An example of God speaking to His people is found in Acts chapter 13:2-3:

> "Whilst they [the church] were worshipping the Lord and fasting, the Holy Spirit said, 'Set apart for me Barnabas and Saul for the work to which I have called them.' So after they had fasted and prayed, they placed their hands on them and sent them off."

The church was already in an atmosphere of prayer and worship, seeking God's will and presence, when God decided to speak to the congregation through the gift of prophecy. God revealed to the Church that He had called Barnabas and Saul to take the good news message to other towns and cities. After receiving God's message, the church prayed for the brothers, who they obeyed and went in response to God's call.

There are countless examples in the Bible of God speaking to His people for God is a God who loves to communicate to us. Let's take a look at some of the main ways that God speaks to His people.

God speaks through the Bible

The most important and readily available means of hearing God's voice is through reading (or listening to) the Bible. God has already spoken on many different subjects in the Bible, so it's the best resource to turn to when we need guidance. If you're unsure where to look, just do a google search. For example, you can search for "Bible verses on encouragement" or "Bible verses on overcoming anxiety." As you read, perhaps a verse will really stand out and speak to your heart. That is God speaking to you and driving home a message by His Spirit through His Word.

Don't underestimate the value and importance of the Bible. It's the most widely distributed book on the planet. According to Wycliffe Bible Translators, 736 languages in the world have access to the full Bible, and another 1658 languages have access to the New Testament, with more translation work going on all the time. There is no other book like it. It is the powerful Word of God, divinely inspired, which has the power to transform lives and communities. The people who wrote it were led by God the Holy Spirit:

> "Above all, you must understand that no prophecy of Scripture came about by the prophet's own interpretation

of things. For prophecy never had its origin in the human will, but prophets, though human, spoke from God as they were carried along by the Holy Spirit." 2 Peter 1:21-22

"All Scripture is God-breathed and is useful for teaching, rebuking, correcting and training in righteousness, so that the servant of God may be thoroughly equipped for every good work." 2 Timothy 3:16-17

In other words, the Bible originated from God and has been given to us to train and equip us to do God's will and purpose. If people lived by the Word of God, it would not only transform our lives for the better, but cities and nations. It is not described as the sword of the Spirit for nothing:

"For the word of God is living and active and full of power [making it operative, energizing, and effective]. It is sharper than any two-edged sword, penetrating as far as the division of the soul and spirit [the completeness of a person], and of both joints and marrow [the deepest parts of our nature], exposing and judging the very thoughts and intentions of the heart." Hebrews 4:12 (Amp)

The Bible is our handbook for life. Whenever you buy something new like a microwave, kettle or even a car, it always comes with a manual to teach you how to use it and what to avoid doing that would damage it. We too have a manual from God, the Bible, our 'go-to' book where we can learn how life best operates and what to avoid that causes harm. The Bible is also our spiritual food. Just as we need to eat physical food every day for our physical strength and wellbeing, so we need to feed ourselves on the Bible for our spiritual strength and sustenance.

On occasions when I've been faced with a particular dilemma whether at work, church, or relationships, and I've not known how to deal with something, I will pray and ask God to show me what to do. I will then just sit in His presence quietly, waiting for Him to guide my thoughts. Often God will bring a Bible verse to mind by His Spirit and through that, provides the much-needed guidance and insight into situations I'm praying about.

God wants to do the same for you. There is already so much teaching from God on many different subjects in the Bible. As you read God's Word, you may find the Holy Spirit impressing a particular verse on your heart. God's Word is the best resource of diving guidance and encouragement.

Do you want to hear from God every day? Then read the Bible every day. Set aside a time each day to do this. Don't just leave it to chance. Schedule it in. Those who read the Bible every day have greater faith, more peace and strength, and a better understanding of God's will for their lives. There is no better substitute than God speaking to us through the Bible. Reading God's Word will enable you to overcome fear, anxiety, depression, and confusion in your life. God will minister to you through His Word and bring healing as you receive it with faith. If you're not sure where to start, begin with the New Testament or the Psalms, or use a Bible reading plan. There are also some great Bible apps for your phone to assist you in reading and understanding God's Word. [3]

God speaks through dreams and visions

In addition to speaking through Scripture, there are many examples in the Bible of God speaking to people through

---

[3] I find the Life Bible, RightNow Media and MessengerX very helpful phone apps.

dreams and visions, revealing His will to them, bringing warnings, or speaking about the future. When God speaks through dreams and visions, it's always for a good reason.

One well known example of God speaking through dreams is found in the story of Joseph:

> "Joseph had a dream, and when he told it to his brothers, they hated him all the more. He said to them, 'Listen to this dream I had: We were binding sheaves of grain out in the field when suddenly my sheaf rose and stood upright, while your sheaves gathered around mine and bowed down to it.'" Genesis 37:5-11

His brothers were already jealous of Joseph as he was the favourite son of their father, exhibited by the beautifully ornamented robe his father had given him. Needless to say, his brothers were not impressed as the dream seemed to infer he would rule over them one day. To make matters worse, he told them a second dream he had:

> "Listen," he said, "I had another dream, and this time the sun and moon and eleven stars were bowing down to me." He told his father as well as his brothers, his father rebuked him and said, 'What is this dream you had? Will your mother and I and your brothers actually come and bow down to the ground before you?' His brothers were jealous of him but his father kept the matter in mind."

Enough was enough and his brothers decided to get rid of their younger brother Joseph and sold him to some passing traders. Torn from his family, his home country and everything familiar, Joseph ended up being sold as a slave in Egypt. There he initially worked for Potiphar, an official for the king of that country. Despite his new status, God was with Joseph, and he prospered in that role. Joseph managed everything so well that Potiphar eventually put his whole household under him. Everything was left under Joseph's care. Things seemed to be improving.

During this period, Joseph gained valuable management experience and leadership skills. God was also working on developing his faith and humility too. However, after some time, Potiphar's wife noticed him and tried numerous times to seduce him, which he rejected and ran from, literally. On one occasion, as he fled from her, he left his cloak on the floor and using that, she concocted a story, falsely accusing Joseph of trying to take advantage of her, the very opposite of what was true. Unfortunately, her husband believed his wife's story, and Joseph was removed from his position and ended up as a prisoner in a dungeon. Yet despite that turn for the worse, even in prison, God was with him, and Joseph was put in charge of all the prisoners. Even in prison, God was preparing Joseph for the great purpose He had once revealed to him through dreams.

Despite the ordeals and distress Joseph suffered, being forcibly removed from his family and everything familiar, Joseph held on to God His dreams. They must have been a great source of hope for Joseph as he walked through the years of trials and injustices.

Despite spending years as a servant and prisoner, God was with Joseph and through those humbling experiences, Joseph learned the necessary skills, character, and trust in God required for the purpose God had for him: Prime Minister of Egypt, second in command to the King. In just one day, Joseph was unexpectedly elevated from dungeon prisoner to Prime Minister because of the wisdom he held and his ability to interpret dreams from God, which were the outworking of his walk with God. In other words, his wisdom from God and spiritual gifts made him stand out amongst his peers and equipped him to fulfil God's purpose for his life.

So Joseph was able to forget all his suffering and God used him to lead Egypt through a very difficult time in history, saving countless lives at a time of great famine. Because of Joseph's wisdom, character, and management skills, which were honed through his previous experiences, he was able to navigate the nation through seven years of bitter famine, providing grain not only for Egypt, but surrounding nations too. When Joseph's own brothers became hungry, they too came down to Egypt, bowed down before the Prime Minister, and asked him for grain for their families and children, fulfilling the dreams God had once given Joseph. Despite how they had treated him, Joseph lovingly provided for his family. God still speaks through dreams today and they can be a powerful encouragement and guidance for our future purpose and everyday life.

An example of God speaking through a vision is found in Acts 10:3-6 when God spoke to a centurion of an Italian Regiment through a vision during a time of prayer:

> "One day at about three in the afternoon he had a vision. He distinctly saw an angel of God, who came to him and said, 'Cornelius!' Cornelius stared at him in fear. 'What is it, Lord?' he asked. The angel answered, 'Your prayers and gifts to the poor have come up as a memorial offering before God. Now send men to Joppa to bring back a man named Simon who is called Peter. He is staying with Simon the tanner, whose house is by the sea.'"

When Simon Peter arrived, he explained the message of the gospel of Jesus Christ to Cornelius and his household, who gladly received the message of salvation and the gift of the Holy Spirit. It was a powerful lesson for Simon Peter and his companions too as God showed them the gospel was not only for the Jews.

Let's look at one more example found in Acts 16:6-10:

> "Paul and his companions travelled throughout the region of Phrygia and Galatia, having been kept by the Holy Spirit from preaching the word in the province of Asia. When they came to the border of Mysia, they tried to enter Bithynia, but the Spirit of Jesus would not allow them to. So they passed by Mysia and went to Troas. During the night Paul had a vision of a man of Macedonia standing and begging him, 'Come over to Macedonia and help us.' After Paul had seen the vision, we got ready at once to leave for Macedonia, concluding that God had called us to preach the gospel to them.'"

Dreams from God occur when we sleep, but a vision is like watching a film either in your mind's eye or visually whilst you're awake. Paul and his companions had been travelling, sharing the gospel and performing signs and wonders. However, when they tried to do so at Mysia, God closed the door. It didn't take long for Paul to find out which door God was opening instead, and when God revealed it to Paul in a vision, he promptly obeyed the call.

God speaks to His people through dreams and visions for many reasons including to provide guidance, revelation of His will for the future, warnings about dangers to pray about, revelation about a harmful situation we may be unaware of, and things to pray about either for ourselves or others. Dreams and visions are a common way that God speaks to His people as the Bible clearly shows.

Years ago, I surrendered my dream life to God and asked Him to speak to me through dreams at night, and He has done that on numerous times since. I find it's a very important way that He guides me. Many of the important decisions I've made about my career and ministry are a result of having dreams as I've sought God in prayer and asked Him to show me His will. Sometimes God will show me something in a dream and I will then pray into that until confirmation and further guidance come from elsewhere. Sometimes God will show me someone to pray for and what His purpose is for their lives, and I just pray into that for them. It's wonderful to see God answer. Dreams and visions then are an effective way that God speaks to us by His Spirit in answer to prayer and can be a great source of hope, encouragement and guidance. Why not ask God to speak to you this way? If you would like to do that, you can pray the following prayer:

> *Almighty God, I thank you that you are a God who desires to speak to us and direct us in the ways we should go. LORD, I give you my dreams. Please speak to me through them and provide me with your guidance. Help me to understand when you speak and follow through in faith and prayer. In the name of Jesus Christ I pray, amen.*

God speaks through words of knowledge

> "Now to each one the manifestation of the Spirit is given for the common good. To one there is given through the Spirit a message of wisdom, to another a message of knowledge by means of the same Spirit." 1 Corinthians 12:7-8.

Words of knowledge can come in the form of actual words coming to mind, or through a strong impression or feeling out of nowhere. There have been times when God has dropped a piece of information into my mind that I know isn't my own. It's always given to help or encourage someone. I've seen God do that in my life to protect others from danger, bring healing to someone, and provide understanding or guidance.

I remember on one occasion when I worked as an associate pastor in Seoul, South Korea, a member of the church asked to meet up, so we met in a coffee shop down town. I had only met her once briefly before. As we talked, suddenly God unexpectedly dropped a piece of knowledge into my mind about her, showing me what her spiritual gifts were. I told her what God had showed me and she was quite surprised. She proceeded to tell me that these were indeed her spiritual gifts but that she hadn't used them for a long time. She felt that God was showing her it was time to start using them again. She was encouraged by God speaking to her that way.

I will share another personal example I will never forget. When I was in my early twenties and a student in Bible college, a friend drove me home late one evening. I lived in a quiet residential area and as it was around midnight, there were hardly any cars on the road. As I was getting out of the car, I suddenly felt an overwhelming impression from God that my friend really needed to be careful driving home that night. It was really strong; I knew it was from God. It took some convincing of my friend that this warning was from God, but he eventually took it on board after a few firm words.

When I saw him the next day, I was eager to hear how his journey home had been the previous night. Excitedly, he proceeded to tell me how he was driving up a hill approaching a blind bend with parked cars on the left side of the road. Normally he would have just overtaken the parked cars, moving into the opposite side of the road. However, because of the warning, he didn't. Even though he didn't see any headlights from oncoming cars coming around the bend, he stopped and gave way behind the parked cars just in case. As he was stopped, a speeding car with no headlights on came speeding down that blind bend on the very side he would have been on had he not stopped and given way! God saved my friend that night from a head on collision, all through a word of knowledge and the prayers for protection by his grandfather, a man of prayer.

God speaks to us through prophecy

> "We have different gifts, according to the grace given to each of us. If your gift is prophesying, then prophesy in accordance with your faith…" Romans 12:6

> "To one there is given through the Spirit a message of wisdom, to another a message of knowledge by means of the same Spirit, to another faith by the same Spirit, to another gifts of healing by that one Spirit, to another miraculous powers, to another prophecy…" 1 Corinthians 12:8-10

Prophecy is basically God providing a message of guidance or instruction from a fellow believer in Christ. Let me share a few examples of what I mean.

When I was in my twenties, I was a student at Bible College. I loved God and desired to work for Him. However, I didn't yet know what that looked like. One weekend, a couple visited our church and the wife had a gift of prophecy and offered to pray for anyone who wanted prayer. I went forward for prayer and when she prayed over me, she gave me a message from God saying that He was going to send me overseas. This was news to me as I had never even thought about moving away, but following that prophetic message, I began to pray about it.

About a year later, a fellow student at Bible College offered me a job in South Korea, and so I began to seek God in prayer as to whether God wanted me to go to that nation. I developed a real peace about going and God spoke to me through His Word and reassured me that He would be with me. By my late twenties I had moved to South Korea where for the next eleven years, God revealed His purpose to me and honed my ministry skills. I joined an excellent English-speaking church ministry and God provided wonderful opportunities to serve Him and grow in ministry. It all began because a sister in Christ gave me a prophetic word.

There have been other times too when God has given a prophetic word of encouragement or comfort from fellow believers who didn't know me or had any idea of what I was experiencing at that time. Prophetic words can be used by God then to bring direction, encouragement, comfort and hope. If God provides you with a message of direction through a prophetic message, pray about that and seek further guidance from God. Test every message to see if it's genuinely from God. Ask God to provide confirmation through His Word and by His Spirit. Take your time and if it's an authentic word from God, He will show you.

Don't be deceived by wrong spirits

I just want to pause here and talk about the dangers of looking to unbiblical and harmful avenues for guidance. Some people, desperate for guidance and encouragement, turn to various forms of fortune telling or divination such as tarot card readings, seances, spiritualist churches, mediums and the like. The Bible makes it clear that such practices are ungodly, inferior and displease God, and we mustn't engage in such activities:

> "When you enter the land the LORD your God is giving you, do not learn to imitate the detestable ways of the nations there. Let no one be found among you who

sacrifices their son or daughter in the fire, who practices divination or sorcery, interprets omens, engages in witchcraft, or casts spells, or who is a medium or spiritist or who consults the dead. Anyone who does these things is detestable to the LORD." Deuteronomy 18:9-12

Pretty strong words. As Isaiah 8:19 says, why consult the dead on behalf of the living? We should inquire of God instead, whose guidance is far better and will do us no harm. If we choose to get guidance from deceiving spirits, we are opening ourselves up to the enemy to mislead and fill us with fear and lead us into harm's way:

"Dear friends, do not believe every spirit, but test the spirits to see whether they are from God, because many false prophets have gone out into the world. This is how you can recognise the Spirit of God: Every spirit that acknowledges that Jesus Christ has come in the flesh is from God, but every spirit that does not acknowledge Jesus is not from God. This is the spirit of the antichrist, which you have heard is coming and even now is already in the world." 1 John 4:1-3

Evil spirits may appear to help, but really what they seek to do is pull us away from God and intimidate us, filling us with fear. The Bible teaches us that there are many spirits in this world not of God and they do not have your best interests at heart despite what they say. They do not know the future, nor do they speak the truth. They may tell you something bad is going to happen, cause you to live in fear about that, and then bring it about. Nor is it your deceased loved one speaking, but a familiar spirit who just knows things about the deceased.

Do not be deceived by these harmful spirits. Those who get involved in such things give a foothold to evil spirits to afflict them and cause problems physically, mentally and spiritually. Whenever I've met someone who dabbles seriously in such things, they are often suffering from physical or mental torment too. It's no surprise. God is not worshipped or present in spiritualist churches, and the children of God should not be attending such places. They are churches of evil and unclean spirits, not God. Don't be misled by the term 'church'. If you have engaged in any activities like that, just confess it to God, repent and ask for His forgiveness in the name of Christ. God loves you and will set you free from ungodly influences, which I will explain more on later in the book.

You have no need to turn to inferior and misleading sources of guidance. God is more than able to give you the guidance you need, which will be far better. Through His Word and by His Holy Spirit, God will answer your prayers and lead and guide you. He will work in your practical circumstances and intervene miraculously. If a door suddenly closes, thank God and ask Him to open us the right one. God has a wonderful purpose for your life and wants to direct you into that.

As we have seen, God wants to speak to you and guide you and He does so through His Word and by His Holy Spirit in different ways. God will never ask you to do something that is contrary to His written Word. Everything God says to us is for our protection, guidance and strengthening. God wants to guide you and show you His will for your family, work, ministry, relationships and fellowship. When what God is saying to you through His Word and Holy Spirit agree, you can be confident of understanding God's will for you. So seek God in prayer and ask Him to speak to you and guide you. As you trust in Him, He will answer you in wonderful ways beyond your imagination:

"Now to him who is able to do immeasurably more than all we ask or imagine, according to his power that is at work within us, to him be glory in the church and in Christ Jesus throughout all generations, for ever and ever! Amen." Ephesians 3:20-21

Questions for further study

1. Have you ever experienced God speaking to you in some way? How did He do that?

2. Have you ever had a dream or vision you think was from God? What was God saying to you?

3. Have you ever received a message of prophecy from someone else? If yes, what was that and how did that impact your life?

4. Please read 2 Timothy 3:16-17. Why is it so important that we regularly read the Bible?

5. Read John 15:5-8. What do you think Jesus is talking about here? How can you apply that to your life?

6. Can you name some people in the Bible who experienced God speaking to them? What did God's guidance achieve?

7. Why do you think turning to fortune telling or divination is wrong?

Part B

Praying through the Lord's Prayer

Chapter 4

Our Father in Heaven, Hallowed be Your name

"In this manner, therefore pray: Our Father in heaven, hallowed be your name. Your kingdom come. Your will be done on earth as it is in heaven. Give us this day our daily bread. And forgive us our debts, as we forgive our debtors. And do not lead us into temptation but deliver us from the evil one. For Yours is the kingdom and the power and the glory forever. Amen." Matthew 6:9-13 (NKJV)

The Lord's Prayer is the most well-known prayer around the world. It is called the Lord's Prayer because it was the Lord Jesus Christ who taught it to His disciples in response to them asking Him to teach them how to pray (Luke 11:1). What many don't realise is, it's a very powerful and all-encompassing prayer. Jesus covers the most important topics pertinent to people's needs, so for the remainder of this book, we will go through it together and delve into its power and effectiveness.

Our Father in heaven

The Lord's Prayer begins by teaching us that when we pray, we do so to God our heavenly Father. Prayer is done in the context of an intimate, loving relationship as God our Father and you His child. Having a heavenly Father might sound strange, but as we have seen, the Bible teaches that God is three Persons in One: God the Father, God the Son (Jesus Christ) and God the Holy Spirit (Matthew 28:19). You may or may not have had a good father growing up, but whatever your experience, when you place your faith in God through Christ, you are adopted as God's child by your heavenly Father who wants to lovingly provide and take care of you, guide you and teach you the best way to go in life. He wants to be the wonderful Father you may have never had:

> "For all who are led by the Spirit of God are sons of God. For you did not receive the spirit of slavery to fall back into fear, but you have received the Spirit of adoption as sons, by whom we cry, 'Abba! Father!' The Spirit himself bears witness with our spirit that we are children of God, and if children, then heirs – heirs of God and fellow heirs with Christ." Romans 8:14-17 (ESV)

The closest English language translation for the word 'Abba' is 'Daddy', the kind of word children use to call their fathers. We find that same word in Galatians 4:6:

> "Because you are his sons, God sent the Spirit of his Son into our hearts, the Spirit who calls out 'Abba, Father.'"

When my earthly father was alive, I used to call him a number of different names: dad, pops, and pappa. They were affectionate names and it reflected a closeness in our relationship. It's the same with God our heavenly Father. We are invited to call Him, 'Abba', and to develop a close relationship with Him for He loves you and wants to bless you as any good father would.

In one of Jesus' most vulnerable moments in His life here on earth, in the Garden of Gethsemane, Jesus addresses His heavenly Father as 'Abba' when He asks Him to take the cup of suffering from Him (Mark 14:36). When Jesus really needed His Father, He called Him Abba. You can approach God your Father in prayer anytime you need Him for He desires to help you:

> "You parents – if your children ask for a loaf of bread, do you give them a stone instead? Of if they ask for a fish, do you give them a snake? Of course not! So if you sinful people know how to give good gifts to your children, how much more will your heavenly Father give good gifts to those who ask him." Matthew 7:9-11 (NLT)

Paul Miller describes the importance and significance of God our Abba Father:

> "We know the word *abba* because it burned itself on the disciples' minds. They were so stunned—no one had spoken to God so intimately before—that when they told the Greek Christians about Jesus, they carried over the Aramaic *abba* into the Greek translations of the Bible. This so shocked Paul that he used *abba* in both Romans and Galatians. Translators have continued the pattern set by the early disciples, and no matter what language Scripture is in, they still use *abba*.
>
> "This one-word prayer, *Father*, is uniquely Jesus' prayer. His first recorded sentence at age twelve is about his father: 'Did you not know that I must be in my Father's house?' (Luke 2:49) *Abba* is the first word the prodigal son utters when he returned home. It is the first word of the Lord's Prayer, and it is the first word Jesus prays in Gethsemane. It is his first word on the cross— 'Father, forgive them' (Luke 23:34)—and one of his last— 'Father, into your hands I commit my spirit!' (Luke 23:46) *Father*

was my first prayer as I began praying continuously, and I find that it is still my most frequent prayer." [4]

No matter what kind of experience you may have had with your earthly father, if you had one at all, your heavenly Father loves and cares for you more than anyone else ever will. As you grow in your relationship with God, He will bring provision and guidance for your needs, and healing into any pain you may carry from past experiences. Your heavenly Father will never leave you nor abandon you. He will never turn his back on you, walk away or ever give up on you:

> "Even if my father and mother abandon me, the LORD will hold me close." Psalm 27:10 (NLT)

> "All who love me will do what I say. My Father will love them, and we will come and make our home with each of them." John 14:23 (NLT)

> "So don't be afraid, little flock. For it gives your Father great happiness to give you the kingdom." Luke 12:32 (NLT)

God holds you in high esteem and believes in you. It's so important that you grasp this: God is your heavenly Father and He invites you to come and talk to him about what's on your heart and what troubles you.

In John 20:17, Jesus told His disciples, *"I am returning to **my Father and your Father**, to my God and your God."* (author's emphasis) The point Jesus was making was that those who become His disciples can also enjoy knowing God as their Father, just as Jesus did. You can be safe and secure in your relationship with Him. As author Greg Ogden describes:

---

[4] Paul Miller, *A Praying Life*, p. 65

PART B

"As adopted children we can enjoy the same favor that Jesus has with the Father. We too are the apple of God's eye, the pleasure of his love, the delight of his focus. And if we didn't get all that we wanted or needed in our human fathers, we are invited even more deeply into the pleasure that the Father of heaven and earth takes in his Son, and us. We have been included in the family and hear the Father say, *'You are my child, whom I love; with you I am well pleased.'* We now have the Father we always needed and wanted." [5]

With your heavenly Father being the Almighty and all-powerful God, He is also able to do something about those needs for you too. He is full of compassion and His love abounds towards you:

"The LORD is compassionate and gracious, slow to anger, abounding in love." Psalm 103:8

As God's child, you have an inheritance and a birth right. We are promised eternal life through faith in Christ and eternal rewards for the good works you do here on earth. We are promised that God our Father will hear and answer our prayers, meet all our needs and even grant the desires of our hearts. I don't know anyone who can love and provide for us like God our Father can:

"See what great love the Father has lavished on us, that we should be called children of God!" 1 John 3:1

God, your Father will never let you down. You can talk to Him about anything. He is completely dependable as I've experienced so many times throughout my life. When you

---

[5] Greg Ogden, *Discipleship Essentials: A Guide To Building Your Life In Christ*, p 116.

have the Creator of the universe on your side, what have you to fear?

> "And when you pray, do not be like the hypocrites, for they love to pray standing in the synagogues and on the street corners to be seen by others. Truly I tell you, they have received their reward in full. But when you pray, go into your room, close the door and pray to your Father, who is unseen. Then your Father, who sees what is done in secret, will reward you. And when you pray, do not keep on babbling like pagans, for they think they will be heard because of their many words. Do not be like them, for your Father knows what you need before you ask him." Matthew 6:5-8

Prayer to God our Father must be sincere, and done in humility and sincerity. You don't have to go to church to pray. You can pray at home, as you walk along the street, drive your car, at work, doing the shopping – anytime and anywhere!

Nor is it about the quantity or eloquence of words. You're not going to impress God just be the sheer length of your prayer or by using fancy words. As Jesus says, God your Father already knows what you need anyway. You may wonder, why bother praying at all then? It's about cultivating the relationship: as you bring your needs and requests before God and then see Him answer your prayers, it does wonders not only for your faith, but it also strengthens your relationship with Him. As you see Him work in your life, you begin to understand that God really does care for you and wants to provide for you. You discover how faithful God is and the power of prayer, and as a result begin to trust Him more and more. It's exciting when you see God answer your prayers. Following God is a real adventure and prayer is a very important part of that. You can pray to God your Father anytime.

Hallowed be your Name

Hallowed essentially means 'holy'. God's name is sanctified, set part, and is unlike any other name on earth. The Bible teaches that God's name must be used in the right way and not as a word of blasphemy as we often hear today. As Exodus 20:7 teaches:

> "You shall not misuse the name of the LORD your God, for the LORD will not hold anyone guiltless who misuses his name."

How we use God's Name is a serious matter. So much so, God included it in his Ten Commandments. The Bible has a lot more to say about God's name.

God's Name is the most powerful name

Speaking about Jesus Christ, in Philippians 2:9-11 we read:

> "And being found in appearance as a man, he humbled himself by becoming obedient to death – even death on a cross! Therefore God exalted him to the highest place and **gave him the name that is above every name**, that at the name of Jesus every knee should bow, in heaven and on earth and under the earth, and every tongue acknowledge that Jesus Christ is Lord, to the glory of God the Father." (author's emphasis)

The Name of Jesus Christ is the highest name, the name above every power and authority you can think of, whether human or spiritual. The Bible teaches that every power has to bow the knee to the name of Christ. There is no other name on earth that is more powerful that Christ's. That also means every sickness, problem and demonic spirit must bow to the name of Jesus Christ. That is very good news indeed!

> "I pray that the eyes of your heart may be enlightened in order that you may know the hope to which he has called you, the riches of his glorious inheritance in his holy people, and his **incomparably great power for us who believe**. That power is the same as the mighty strength he exerted when he raised Christ from the dead and **seated him at his right hand in the heavenly realms, far above all rule and authority, power and dominion, and every name that is invoked**, not only in the present age but also in the one to come. **And God placed all things under his feet**…" Ephesians 1:18-22 (author's emphasis)

Those are some very powerful verses, teaching that Christ is over all and that the same incomparable power that raised Him from the dead is available to us. This is why Christ's name is the most powerful name, for He is over all.

If someone brought a request on behalf of King Charles, the receiver would have to obey because the King's name is the most powerful authority in the land. The King's name represents his power and position, and as his subjects, we would have to comply. How much more with the King of Kings, Jesus Christ? Here are some important Bible verses that explain what can be done in the most powerful name of Jesus Christ:

> The seventy-two [disciples] returned with joy and said, "Lord, even the demons submit to us in your name." Luke 10:17

> "Stretch out your hand to heal and perform signs and wonders through the name of your holy servant Jesus." Acts 4:30

"Salvation is found in no one else, for there is no other name under heaven given to mankind by which we must be saved." Acts 4:12

"Everyone who calls on the name of the Lord will be saved." Romans 10:13

"Very truly I tell you, whoever believes in me will do the works I have been doing, and they will do even greater things that these, because I am going to the Father. And I will do whatever you ask in my name, so that the Father may be glorified in the Son. You may ask me for anything in my name, and I will do it." John 14:12-14

"And these signs will accompany those who believe: In my name they will drive out demons; they will speak in new tongues; they will pick up snakes with their hands; and when they drink deadly poison, it will not hurt them at all; they will place their hands on sick people, and they will get well." Mark 16:17-18

"Until now you have not asked for anything in my name. Ask and you will receive, and your joy will be complete." John 16:24

Stop for a few minutes and think about what those verses are promising. They have the power to change your life. We pray in Christ's name for it is through Christ we can approach God our Father in prayer. Christ died for our sin on the cross and we are therefore forgiven and receive salvation as we repent and place our faith in Christ. But the blessings don't stop there. That's just the start! In Christ's name we can also pray for healing, deliverance and anything else you need.

We pray in Christ's name because that's where the power and privilege originates. Christ's name brings salvation, healing, deliverance and all kinds of signs and wonders. Christ has this power because when He rose from the dead, after dying on the cross for our sins and sicknesses, He conquered the power of the Devil, including sin and death as Colossians 2:13-15 (NLT) explains:

> "You were dead because of your sins and because your sinful nature was not yet cut away. Then God made you alive with Christ, for he forgave all our sins. He cancelled the record of the charges against us and took it away by nailing it to the cross. In this way, **he disarmed the spiritual rulers and authorities.** He shamed them publicly by his **victory over them on the cross**." (author's emphasis)

When someone is disarmed, their weapons and power are forcibly removed. They are defeated and conquered and become powerless. This is what happened when Christ died for our sins and rose from the dead: He disarmed and defeated the powers of evil spiritual rulers and authorities. The enemy is defeated and is a conquered foe. We are on the winning side and Christ's name is over all. Our adversary, the Devil, knows this and unfortunately does a good job in leading people to think Christ's name is just the opposite, a mere word of blasphemy. However, through these scriptures, we learn the truth, that Christ's name is the most powerful name on all the earth, which can accomplish what no other name can: salvation, healing and deliverance, making us whole.

Understand therefore the power and sanctity of His name and pray in the almighty name of Jesus Christ. Hallowed and powerful be His name.

PART B

Questions for further study

1. How do you feel knowing that God is your heavenly Father? What difference should that make to your life?

2. Have you ever experienced the power of Christ's name?

3. Read 1 John 3:1. What do we learn about God's love for us through this verse? What do you think that means?

4. Read 2 Corinthians 6:14-18. What do you learn about God's will regarding relationships in your life?

5. Why do you think God teaches this?

6. What does God promise for those who obey?

7. Now read Luke 6:35-36. What do we learn about God's Father heart towards us from these verses?

Chapter 5

Your kingdom come. Your will be done on earth as it is in heaven

Your Kingdom come

Continuing in the Lord's Prayer, Jesus next taught us to pray for God's kingdom to come, a subject he talked a lot about:

"Truly I tell you, I will not drink again from the fruit of the vine until that day when I drink it new in the kingdom of God." Mark 14:25

"Very truly, I tell you, no one can see the kingdom of God unless they are born again." John 3:3

There are a number of aspects of the kingdom of God, one being an eternal destination where God dwells and where those who are born again will one day enter (also referred to it as the kingdom of heaven). Jesus taught that it is better to enter the kingdom of God with one eye than to have both eyes, live a sinful life and be thrown into hell. The kingdom of God then is it is a future destination to be desired, no matter what the cost.

An additional aspect is that the kingdom of God can also be experienced here on earth. It's not just about eternity:

> The coming of the kingdom of God is not something that can be observed, nor will people say, "Here it is," or "There it is," because the kingdom of God is in your midst. Luke 17:20-21

> But if it is by the Spirit of God that I drive out demons, then the kingdom of God has come upon you. Matthew 12:28

These verses indicate that the kingdom of God is a reality that we can experience on earth.

The kingdom of God is the manifestation of God's power and presence here on earth

Jesus taught us that we need to pray for the kingdom of God to come to earth, for when it does, God's power and presence manifests and brings salvation and meets needs. God's kingdom power sets people free from all forms of sickness and evil that oppresses them, and leads us to the knowledge of God. When God's kingdom comes, God's light forces darkness out. American Pastor Bill Johnson explains Matthew 12:28:

> Look at the phrase, "by the Spirit of God…the kingdom." The Holy Spirit encompasses the Kingdom. While they are not the same, they are inseparable. The Holy Spirit enforces the lordship of Jesus, marking His territory with liberty. The king's domain becomes evident through his work.
> The second part of this verse reveals the nature of ministry. Anointed ministry causes the collision of two worlds – the world of darkness with the world of light.

> This passage shows the nature of deliverance. When the Kingdom of God comes upon someone, powers of darkness are forced to leave…
> Those who learn to work with the Holy Spirit actually cause the reality of His world (His dominion) to collide with the powers of darkness that have influence over a person or situation.[6]

The whole message of Jesus Christ centred on the coming of the kingdom of God to earth. Jesus said, "I must proclaim the good news of the kingdom of God to the other towns also, because that is why I was sent." (Luke 4:43) Jesus preached the kingdom of God, confirming His message through His teachings and all the miracles He performed. However, His mission didn't stop there.

Called to continue God's kingdom work

When Jesus returned to heaven, He commanded us, His followers, to continue the same work and preach the same message:

> "He [Jesus] said to them, 'Go into all the world and preach the gospel to all creation. Whoever believes and is baptised will be saved, but whoever does not believe will be condemned. And these signs will accompany those who believe: In my name they will drive out demons; they will speak in new tongues; they will pick up snakes with their hands; and when they drink deadly poison, it will not hurt them at all; they will place their hands on sick people, and they will get well." Mark 16:15-18

---

[6] Bill Johnson: *When Heaven Invades Earth: A Practical Guide to a Life of Miracles*, p. 73.

The kingdom of God then is a reality to be prayed for and sought after *now*, made manifest through our faith and our obedience. Christ called His followers to continue spreading the message of God's kingdom, saving the lost, healing the sick and setting free the oppressed. Two friends, Jeremy and Scala, have dedicated their lives to Christ's call. On one mission trip to remote villages in India some years ago, they and their team experienced the reality of God's kingdom's power:

> We were in South India, in a small village area called Dharma Puri. We had already been to a couple of villages that day sharing the gospel, and this was our last before returning home. Our programmes consisted of worship dances, dramas, and preaching, with a time to pray for the sick. As soon as we started our dances, everyone on our team suddenly had pain in their feet. We were used to having sore feet, but this time was different. But we trudged through and eventually got to the end.
> As we asked people to come up for prayer, a woman approached me and my wife. She told us that she had been having severe stomach pains. We laid our hands on her to pray, and immediately she fell to the ground shaking and her eyes rolled back in her head. It's easy enough to recognise when an evil spirit is oppressing someone. This woman was a Hindu and did not yet believe in Jesus. As we continued to pray for her, we found out a local witch doctor had placed a curse on her. We continued to pray but the pain only lessened; it did not leave. Eventually we ran out of time and had to leave. A few days later was Sunday, and she came to morning church service with her husband and son. She was still feeling pain in her stomach, but during the service they decided to ask Jesus into their lives. As we prayed with her, they all accepted Jesus into their hearts and suddenly

the pain was gone! After we left India, they continued to send us letters for several years. God has given her freedom and new life.

We need to pray for God's kingdom to come because there is another kingdom also at work here on earth: that of the Devil. The two are clearly distinguishable. The Devil's kingdom is manifest through evil, sickness, death and destruction, whereas God's kingdom is manifest in goodness, healing, life and salvation. Jeremy and Scala's testimony illustrates what God's kingdom manifest on earth looks like: bringing life, healing and salvation, overcoming the kingdom of the Devil. This is all possible because Christ overcame all the power of the evil one through his death and resurrection as we read earlier.

The power of God's kingdom manifest

God desires that His kingdom power and values be manifest through our lives. It's not just an eternal destination. God's kingdom has not changed. His desire for mankind to experience and receive His healing and salvation has not altered. Everything Jesus taught – how to receive salvation from our sins and enter eternity, how to know God, love our neighbour, walk in His amazing purposes for our lives, grow in maturity and goodness, and experience God's powerful healing and deliverance - is all part of His wonderful kingdom message. This is what Jesus Himself taught and His message is still completely relevant and needed more than ever in our hurting and broken world. We are not only to pray for God's kingdom to come, but we are also called to be instruments whom God can use to bring His kingdom to earth, just as the early Christ followers were:

> "When Jesus had called the Twelve together, he gave them power and authority to drive out all demons and to cure diseases, and he sent them out to proclaim the kingdom of God and to heal the sick." Luke 9:1-2

> "Peter said, 'Silver or gold I do not have, but what I do have I give you. In the name of Jesus Christ of Nazareth, walk.' Taking him by the right hand, he helped him up, and instantly the mans' feet and ankles became strong. He jumped to his feet and began to walk." Acts 3:6-8

> "The apostles performed many signs and wonders among the people…As a result, people brought the sick into the streets and laid them on beds and mats so that at least Peter's shadow might fall on some of them as he passed by. Crowds gathered also from the towns around Jerusalem, bringing their sick and those tormented by impure spirits, and all of them were healed." Acts 5:12, 15-16

> "Paul entered the synagogue and spoke boldly there for three months, arguing persuasively about the kingdom of God." Acts 19:8

Before His departure, Jesus said,

> "Very truly I tell you, **whoever believes in me will do the works I have been doing, and they will do even greater things than these**, because I am going to the Father. And I will do whatever you ask in my name, so that the Father may be glorified in the Son. You may ask me for anything in my name, and I will do it." John 14:12–14 (author's emphasis)

That 'whoever' includes you and I. These are amazing promises.

Any person who follows Christ as their Lord and Saviour can do the works Jesus did.

The Early Christians preached the good news of the kingdom of God and miracles followed. People's physical and spiritual needs were met, and they continue to be met as God's mission is fulfilled all over the world today.

We are called to pray for God's kingdom to come, that God's power and love will be manifest in people's lives. That people will be saved, healed and set free from whatever oppresses them. That the teaching of Christ's truth which brings life will be taught. Signs and miracles confirm the gospel message of forgiveness and salvation, showing people that God is real and that He loves and cares for them. The world desperately needs God's love and healing power. As 1 Corinthians 4:20 says: "For the kingdom of God does not consist in talk but in power." (ESV)

Pray for God's kingdom to come in your own life, the lives of your loved ones and those you meet. As you do, you are praying for the very presence and power of God's kingdom to come, defeating the power of evil, and transforming lives. Our loved ones still need saving, healing, and freedom from what oppresses them. Pray boldly and in faith in the name of Jesus Christ.

Your will be done

Why did Jesus teach us to pray for God's kingdom to come and for His will to be done? Isn't God's will always being done? It would appear not for why else would He command us to pray this way?

Hand on heart, have you always obeyed God's will in your life? I wish I could say that I've been 100% obedient, but I haven't. The fact is, God's will isn't always being done.

However if we walked in obedience to God's will more, we'd see God move more in our lives.

Walking in God's will

> "This is the confidence we have in approaching God: that if we ask anything according to his will, he hears us. And if we know that he hears us – whatever we ask – we know that we have what we asked of him." 1 John 5:14

Do you want to follow God's will in your life? It's a challenging question and in my experience as a church pastor, I have seen a variety of responses. The problem is, by nature, we want to make our own decisions and following God's will can seem like a foreign concept. We may include God's will as one of the options to consider, but when it boils down to it, we prefer to follow our own plans and desires. However, living by that method will lead to missing out on God's very best plan for your life.

For some who've humbly admit that they've made poor choices in the past, choosing God's will is something they really want to do. They've realised God's will is bound to be better than their own, so no matter what direction God guides them in, it's a yes. Such people experience the real blessings of going God's way.

God has given us free will. He has given us the freedom to make our own decisions and to choose whether to pursue His will in our lives or our own. God knows and sees everything: the end from the beginning, the motives of everyone's hearts, and He knows what's going to happen tomorrow. He is all wise and all loving and has our best interests at heart. Given these facts, it would be wise to seek God's will and follow that. I have found it to be the very best thing we can do. I am quite happy to admit that I don't have the wisdom, networks or knowledge I need to put myself in healthy or safe environments where I can best flourish. But God does, and it's prudent and sensible to seek what God's will is and follow that, and as 1 John 5:14 promises, when we pray according to God's will, He will hear and answer us.

When things go wrong

Don't get me wrong: walking in God's will isn't a fail-safe from things going pear shaped. Despite trying to follow God's will in my life, there have been a few occasions where people I've partnered or worked with do not want to follow God's will and as a result I have found myself in some very unexpected and painful situations. Even so, when I seek God in those moments, He shows me the way forward, delivers me and leads me into victory. Even though we may be blindsided by things that happen, God never is and prepares a way for us ahead of time. God is a God of justice and He never lets people get away with doing wrong to His children for too long. He will always intervene and rescue His people from those who seek to harm them. Sometimes His rescue can be pretty dramatic.

God can bring great good and blessing out of the worst of situations, plundering the enemy's camp. God will always lead you into victory as you follow His will. As Jesus taught, the enemy comes to steal, kill and destroy, but He came to give us life to the full (John 10:10). God's way is always the best way as Romans 12:2 confirms,

> "Do not conform to the pattern of this world, but be transformed by the renewing of your mind. Then you will be able to test and approve what God's will is – **his good, pleasing and perfect will**." (author's emphasis)

Are there any decisions in life you've made that you regret? A relationship you wish you had stayed away from?

An act you wish you hadn't done? We've all been there. Sometimes that might be because we didn't know what someone was really like, or what we were getting ourselves in to. Whatever the reason, we all need help with our choices in life because what we want and desire isn't always good for us, and we may not realise it at the time.

God wants the best for you and to guide you in making decisions. He wants you to know what His plans are for your life, and as you pray to God and seek His will, He will reveal those to you. Then, according to 1 John 5:14, if we ask for something that is in line with God's will, He hears and answers our prayers. We therefore need to seek God in prayer to learn what God's will is and follow that for according to Romans 12:2, God's will is good, pleasing and perfect. It's the best path to follow. I have personally found God's plan to be the most exciting way to live. God has led me in directions I could never have imagined for myself. It may require taking some steps of faith and even sacrifices, but nothing compares to following God's will for our lives.

How to learn God's will

So how do we discover God's will for our lives? The most important means is through reading the Bible. God's will is already revealed about many different subjects in His book. For example, dealing with relationships, how to make a difference in this world, the importance of honesty and integrity and so on. You can learn much about the will of God from reading the Bible.

Set aside time to seek God's will

As we read the Bible, we will discover what God's will is on many subjects. That's where the transformation begins, by replacing those dark and negative thoughts with the truth and light of God's Word. It's hard to stop negative thoughts; it's easier to replace them with the positive teachings of the Bible. This is how transformation begins. Start your day by spending time reading God's Word and talking to God about what's on your heart and mind. If you're more of a night person, then night may work best for you. Whatever time you choose, reading God's Word and prayer will put positive and encouraging thoughts into your mind, pushing any negative ones aside.

> *Seeking God through reading the Bible and prayer will be the most beneficial things you can do for your life*

I have found seeking God through reading the Bible and prayer to be the most beneficial things to do for my life. As I spend time with God, He speaks to my heart and challenges and changes my negative thinking, bringing encouragement and hope. God's Word will also guide you through various difficulties, giving you the comfort and counsel you need. It's the best footing to start each day. I highly recommend it.

Many of us are busy. I work full time plus I oversee a charity, and so I need to get up early to make sure I prioritise time to spend with God. When I write, I need to get up even earlier, between 4.30am and 5.30am just to make sure I have time to fit everything in. I go to bed around 9.30pm or 10pm, and I find that's enough sleep.

Getting up early to spend quality time with God will put you in a good frame of mind for the day ahead and will help protect your heart and mind from worry and fear. These daily disciplines are foundational for successfully walking with God. As with many things in life, you get out what you put in.

Spending time with God each day is how you develop your friendship with God. It's how you begin to recognise His voice. How can you know God and His will and purpose for you if you don't give Him time and space to speak to you? God wants to teach and guide you. He wants to encourage and strengthen you, and help you make better choices. Sometimes that will mean letting go of our own desires to make room for His better decisions. I have learned that it's of great benefit to ask God what His will is for my life and to follow that, rather than asking Him to bless my own inferior choices.

God is good and His will for you will better any plan you can come up with for yourself. Ask God what His will is for you for as the Bible teaches, He has good plans for your life:

> "For I know the plans I have for you," declares the LORD, "plans to prosper you and not to harm you, plans to give you hope and a future." Jeremiah 29:11

God knows you better than you know yourself and He knows how you will best function and be satisfied in life. As Ephesians 2:10 (NLT) says:

> "For we are God's masterpiece. He has created us anew in Christ Jesus, so we can do the good things he planned for us long ago."

You're His masterpiece. All the talents, skills, and dreams He's put in you: these are all part of your purpose DNA for you. God already planned long ago the purpose and good works He wants you to do. It's already all formed in His heart and mind, so be encouraged to seek His will and trust Him when He guides you in a particular direction you may not have imagined.

Jesus Christ learned surrender

Even Jesus learned to surrender His will to the will of God His Father. In the Garden of Gethsemane, the hour before the arrest which led to His crucifixion, Jesus poured out His heart to His Father, and asked Him to save Him from the painful death He knew He was about to experience. In Matthew 26:39, we read:

> "Going a little farther, he fell with his face to the ground and prayed, 'My Father, if it is possible, may this cup be taken from me. Yet not as I will, but as you will.'"

Jesus was asking His Father if there was any other way to fulfil His plan for salvation for mankind other than having to go to the cross. Through His prayer, He realised that there was no other way, so He obediently surrendered Himself to His Father's will. He understood that He was dying in the place of the world, taking our punishment upon Himself, so we could receive forgiveness and be reconciled to God our Father. However, He also knew death wasn't the end for Him. Hebrews 12:2 talks about the joy Jesus saw beyond the cross:

> "For the joy set before him he endured the cross, scorning its shame, and sat down at the right hand of the throne of God."

He knew His Father could save Him from death, and He knew that because of the time He spent praying to His Father:

> "During the days of Jesus' life on earth, he offered up prayers and petitions with fervent cries and tears to the one who could save him from death, and he was heard because of his reverent submission. Son though he was, he learned obedience from what he suffered and once made perfect, he became the source of eternal salvation for all who obey him." Hebrews 5:7-9

Because He was willing to submit to the Father's great plan, Jesus was saved from death (He rose up from the grave three days later), and His sacrifice made it possible for everyone who believes in Him to experience life and salvation.

Allow God to transform you

> "Do not conform to the pattern of this world, but be transformed by the renewing of your mind. Then you will be able to test and approve what God's will is – his good, pleasing and perfect will." Romans 12:2

I don't know about you, but if I spend too much time scrolling through social media feeds or watching the news, I soon feel it's negative influence in my thinking. Matthew 6:22 teaches that the eye is the lamp of the body and if we allow our eyes to feast on too much negativity through our digital devices, we soon feel it's influence.

How the world thinks and how God thinks are very different. The world is full of compromise and indulgence, which are counter to the values of God's kingdom. The Bible teaches that if we want to discern God's will, then we need to allow God to renew our mind and transform our thinking as Romans 12:2 explains.

Transformation happens by changing the way we think

How we think has a huge impact upon how we live our lives for every action and decision we make begins in our thought life. Fixate too much on negative experiences and influences, and you will soon feel it's effect. Our thought life influences everything we say and do. You are what you think:

PART B

> "For as he thinks in his heart, so is
> he." Proverbs 23:7 (NKJV)

Author and preacher, Joyce Meyer, says, "where the mind goes, the man follows." However, our minds are sometimes not very healthy grounds, and we don't always understand the relationship between our thought life and our actions, attitudes and decisions. For many of us, our thought life needs some transformation. I recommend Joyce Meyer's book, *The Mind Connection*, which explains this in more detail. She has a powerful story of how God changed her life for the better by changing how she thought. She had experienced fifteen years of sexual abuse by her father as a child so you can imagine what that did to her physically, emotionally and mentally. As a result, she admits she spent many years angry and cranky. However, she came to know God and slowly God transformed her, beginning with her thinking. God transformed her life and today she is a very well-known teacher and has written many books, helping others experience the positive change, healing and transformation that she experienced. As Ephesians 2:22-24 emphasises:

> "You were taught, with regard to your former way of life, to put off your old self, which is being corrupted by its deceitful desires; to be made new in the attitude of your minds, and to put on the new self, created to be like God in true righteousness and holiness."

According to these verses, we are made new as our mind is renewed. Spending time reading God's Word and in prayer are key in facilitating that positive change and transformation. God's Word is full of truth and hope and as you saturate your mind with God's truth, you will feel it's positive affect. God will change your thinking for the better, and then you will be able to discern and understand what God's will is for your life and make better decisions.

Pursue and pray for God's will

> "Seek first the kingdom of God and his righteousness, and all these things will be added to you." Matthew 6:33

You cannot follow God's plan and will for your life whilst pursuing your own agenda. Perhaps God has put a dream in your heart. If that's the case, trust His ways and timing. He will fulfil that in your life as your seek Him, trust and obey Him. He will open doors when He knows you're ready.

God's plans for you are bigger and better than anything you can imagine for yourself and following Him can be a real adventure. God has led me to places and work that I could never have dreamed up for myself. Doing life with God, following His will and plan, is far more fulfilling than following your own. Pray and seek God's kingdom and His will first in your life and you will see God do great things and supply all you need to fulfil His purpose.

On earth as it is in heaven

In heaven, where God dwells, God's will is always being done as you would expect. However, down here on our planet earth, that's a different story. As already mentioned, news feeds daily show countless stories of suffering, evil, sickness and hopelessness, none of which is God's will. Jesus came to bring life to the full and evil and suffering are opposite to that and therefore not God's will. So what is the answer?

It begins by praying for God's kingdom to come and for His will to be done *here on earth as it is in heaven,* for as we do, we are praying for God's presence and power to come from heaven to earth. God is the only One who can truly heal the sickness in our world, and we can partner with Him in His work through prayer.

Pray for God's presence and power to come and manifest here on earth

God's will here on earth comes in the form of restoration of broken relationships, miraculous provisions, and physical and emotional healing. God's kingdom brings life and salvation, together with healing and freedom from all kinds of sicknesses (however hopeless), oppression, depression, addiction, compulsions, and mental ill-heath.

When Jesus walked the earth He healed people from all kinds of physical and spiritual afflictions. This same work is needed more than ever today. Healing and setting people free from the work of unclean spirits was a huge part of Jesus' ministry. The need for healing and liberation has not changed. From personal experience in pastoral ministry and from speaking to healing evangelists, I would say around 50% of illnesses, both physical and mental, are caused by unclean, evil spirits afflicting people. That might sound like a shocking statement, but since Jesus spent so much time removing the influence of unclean spirits from people's lives, why would it be any different now? If anything, there are many more opportunities for unclean spirits to influence people given all the violence, hatred, lying, greed, murder, sexual immorality, and witchcraft that's pervasive in movies, computer games and programmes.

Don't underestimate the impact that these negative influences can have upon us mentally, spiritually and emotionally, whatever our age, including children. The good news is, God is able to set us free.

God's kingdom and will being done here on earth then comes not only in the form of confidence of eternal salvation but also in God setting people free from all kinds of fears, anxiety, nightmares, sickness, depression, suicidal thoughts, and voices in our heads. God can set you completely free and bring healing if you experience any of those.

God wants His kingdom to come and His will to be done here on earth. God has provided the means for you and I to experience His power through what His Son, Jesus Christ, did for us. You can have great hope in God. You absolutely have a future, no matter what you've been through and survived, or what you might have done. Remember what Jesus said in John 10:10 (ESV):

> "The thief comes only to steal and kill and destroy. I came that they may have life and have it abundantly."

Jesus came to give you a full and abundant life

That's God's plan for you: to give you a full and abundant life. The enemy's plan however is the opposite: to destroy us. You get to choose which happens, and if you choose to follow God's will for your life, He can then use you to help others find the full and abundant life they also need.

Pray therefore for God's kingdom to come and His will to be done here on earth in your life and your loved ones. God is all powerful and almighty and nothing is impossible for Him.

PART B

Questions for further study

1. In your own words, why is it important that we pray for God's kingdom to come here on earth?

2. Have you ever prayed for God's will to be done in your life?

3. Have you ever sought God's will on something and experienced God's guidance as a result? If yes, what was that? Did you obey?

4. What do you think it means to seek first God's kingdom and His righteousness (Matthew 6:33)?

5. Do you find yourself succumbing to negative thoughts too much in your life?

6. Are there any negative influences in your life that you think need addressing and possibly removing? If yes, what are they?

7. Has this chapter highlighted an area in your life that needs God's touch? If yes, what is that?

Chapter 6

Give us this day our daily bread

Daily bread in the Lord's Prayer represents our everyday practical needs, and the Bible teaches that God promises to provide our needs as we ask Him for His provision. There are many wonderful accounts in the Bible where God miraculously provided for His people. From the provision of daily manna from heaven for forty years for the Israelites wandering in the desert to Jesus feeding a hungry crowd of five thousand with a couple of loaves of bread and a few fish, God has been miraculously providing for His people in the most unexpected ways and continues to do so today. One of my favourite stories of God's provision is for a poor widow who was broke and bankrupt:

> "The wife of a man from the company of the prophets cried out to Elisha, 'Your servant my husband is dead, and you know that he revered the LORD. But now his creditor is coming to take my two boys as his slaves.'
> Elisha replied to her, 'How can I help you? Tell me, what do you have in your house?' 'Your servant has nothing there at all,' she said,' except a small jar of olive oil.'
> Elisha said, 'Go around and ask all your neighbours for empty jars. Don't ask for just a few. Then go inside and shut the door behind you and your sons. Pour oil into all the jars, and as each is filled, put it to one side.'

She left him and shut the door behind her and her sons. They brought the jars to her and she kept pouring. When all the jars were full, she said to her son, 'Bring me another one.'
But he replied, 'There is not a jar left. Then the oil stopped flowing.
She went and told the man of God, and he said, 'Go, sell the oil and pay your debts. You and your sons can live on what is left.'" 2 Kings 4:1-7

Often when God provides, there is an element of faith required on our part, which we see at work in this story. It took faith for the woman to listen to Elisha and ask her neighbours for empty jars. I'm sure they would have asked her what she wanted them for. The act of pouring oil the last remaining jar of oil into empty jars was also a step of faith. I would have been tempted to keep it for our last meals but she believed the prophetic word from the man of God and obeyed, and reaped the reward for her faith. God is so faithful when we operate in faith.

As for many reading these words, there have been numerous moments in my life where I lacked finances and needed God's provision. Whether that's been to pay for daily necessities, college fees, car breakdowns, utility bills or furniture, God has been faithful and has often miraculously provided.

Car repair

I remember one instance of God's miraculous provision when I was in my late twenties, studying full time and working part time on weekends just to try to make ends meet. I was living on my own and had no other support, so it was a struggle. One Friday morning, my employer rang and informed me that they had overcharged me on tax and that they were going to refund me £300 into my bank account that afternoon. Needless to say, I was happy to hear that news and started thinking what I could use it for.

On my way home from University later that day, as I was nearing my home, my car suddenly started making a very loud noise in the engine. Instead of turning into my street, I instead slowly but carefully rolled my car down the bottom of the hill where my local garage was situated. I managed to get it there and was told to come back the next day after they'd taken a look. The next day, the garage owner gave me the news. A gasket had gone and it was not going to be cheap. Remembering my phone call from my employer the day before, I knew how much it was going to cost before he told me and stood there with a big smile on my face. He must have thought me strange as he gave me the news: it was going to cost £300.

College Fees

When I was 22, God called me to study at Bible College but at the time, I had no finances. My family had no resources to provide for me either so I was really on my own in my venture. I not only needed to cover the cost of tuition fees, but I also accommodation, travel and other daily necessities. What was I to do? I sought the Lord earnestly in prayer. Was it really His will for me to go? How was I going to find the money to pay for everything? I held off accepting the college offer until I had further direction from God.

One day I was looking in the mirror when God dropped Philippians 4:19 into my mind. I looked up the verse to see what it said:

> "And my God will meet all your needs according to the riches of his glory in Christ Jesus."

I knew God had spoken and understood what He was saying: go to college in faith and He will provide. That was enough for me so I accepted their offer and went. Nothing had changed when I went to college. No money had miraculously appeared in my bank account so it was a step of faith to go. But over the months and years, I saw God provide in different ways. I studied in that college for four and a half years. I joined an employment agency and worked whatever part time jobs I could, from cleaning toilets to doing office work, and when I couldn't make up the rest, God provided miraculously. I graduated without owing anything to the College. Only He could have done that. I did my part by studying and working hard, and He did the rest through His miraculous provisions for what I lacked.

If I hadn't gone to college in faith but just waited until the monies came in first, it wouldn't have happened. God loves it when we take Him at His Word and operate in faith, for doing so releases God's power.

Moving in faith moves God's power

In Mark 11:24, Jesus made a promise:

"Therefore I tell you, whatever you ask for in prayer, believe that you have received it, and it will be yours."

In other words, we need to take God at His Word in faith and move forward.

Principles of prayer

God invites us to bring all our burdens and needs to Him in prayer, whether that's for financial provision, a new job, monthly bills, guidance for the future, help with a relationship, or for healing. God can meet our every need and it begins with the prayer of faith, taking God at His

Word, trusting Him for His provision and intervention as James 5 explains:

> "Is anyone among you in trouble? Let them pray. Is anyone happy? Let them sing songs of praise. Is anyone among you sick? Let them call the elders of the church to pray over them and anoint them with oil in the name of the Lord. **And the prayer offered in faith will make the sick person well**; the Lord will raise them up. If they have sinned, they will be forgiven. Therefore confess your sins to each other so that you may be healed. **The prayer of a righteous person is powerful and effective**. Elijah was a human being, even as we are. He prayed earnestly that it would not rain, and it did not rain on the land for three and a half years. Again he prayed, and the heavens gave rain, and the earth produced its crops." James 5:13-18 (author's emphasis)

Here we find two important principles that are influential in seeing our prayers answered: the need to pray in faith, and the need to walk in righteousness. Let's take a closer look at each of these.

What faith looks like

Verse 15 promises that the prayer offered in faith will make the sick person well. But what does the prayer of faith look like? Operating in faith is not as foreign as we might at first think. All of us use faith every day without realising we're doing it. When you sit on a chair, you have confidence it will hold you and not collapse. That's essentially operating in faith. When you get on a plane, you trust the pilots will get you to your destination safely. That is also operating by faith. If you do a job of work, you believe your employer will pay you at the end of the month. We already move in faith in our everyday lives without realising it. It's about having confidence and expectation that someone will do something for you, and acting on that confidence.

Having faith in God is no different: you are confident He will do as He promises, meet your needs, and therefore you act on His promises in faith. Our words and actions need to reflect our faith in God. Hebrews 11:1 provides an excellent definition of faith:

> Now faith is the **substance** of things hoped for, the **evidence** of things not seen. (NKJV; author's emphasis)

In this definition, two key words provide crucial insight into what faith looks like: *substance* and *evidence*. Those two words show us that faith is more than just belief. It needs to translate into action. There needs to be substance and evidence to what we believe:

Substance = physical matter
Evidence = demonstration of existence

Faith that sees answers to prayer moves from just passive belief into active demonstration. Faith needs to have substance to it and moving in that kind of faith releases God's power. The sitting on the chair and the getting on the plane is the substance of your faith and confidence. If you weren't willing to step out in faith and get on the plane or sit on the chair, you wouldn't get anywhere. Faith that releases God's power then is more than belief. It goes beyond that into substance and evidence. Reflect on that. Let's look at a Biblical example.

The woman healed from bleeding

> "As Jesus was on his way, the crowds almost crushed him. And a woman was there who had been subject to

bleeding for twelve years, but no one could heal her. She came up behind him and touched the edge of his cloak, and immediately her bleeding stopped. 'Who touched me?' Jesus asked. When they all denied it, Peter said, 'Master, the people are crowding and pressing against you.' But Jesus said, '**Someone touched me; I know that power has gone out from me.**' Then the woman, seeing that she could not go unnoticed, came trembling and fell at his feet. In the presence of all the people, she told why she had touched him and how she had been instantly healed. Then he said to her, '**Daughter, your faith has healed you.** Go in peace.'" Luke 8:42–48 (author's emphasis)

What I love about this passage is that even Jesus didn't see the miracle coming. The woman initiated the miracle, not Jesus. She knew that if she just touched Jesus' cloak, she would be healed and so she pressed through the crowd, reached out her hand in faith and touched Jesus' cloak. That simple act of faith dramatically released God's power and she was instantly healed.

Many of us stand off the side, metaphorically speaking, wondering whether God wants to heal us at all, and just wait and pray, hoping He will have mercy. However, that kind of thinking does not reflect what the Bible teaches about God's will to heal and how to operate in faith. This woman was desperate and literally reached out in faith and as a result, was healed. Even Jesus was surprised by the release of power.

Faith that has substance releases God's power

Faith that has substance to it is releases God's power needed for your miracle. It is God's will to heal. We need to operate in faith. Here are some further promises of God answering prayers of faith given by Jesus Christ:

> "If you believe, you will receive whatever you ask for in prayer." Matthew 21:22

> Jesus said, "Therefore I tell you, whatever you ask for in prayer, believe that you have received it, and it will be yours." Mark 11:24

I love this verse in Mark 11. I call it 'forward faith'. Jesus taught that when we pray, we need to believe God has already answered. If you believe that God has answered, we might not see it yet with our physical eyes, but we 'see' it with our spiritual eyes and our actions and words will reflect that. Let me share a true story of what this kind of faith in God looks like from the book *Faith Like Potatoes*.

South African farmer Angus Buchan shares his journey to trusting God and believing Him for the impossible. One year his and all the surrounding farmlands were experiencing a particularly fierce drought, so much so that no one had planted anything ready for the coming season. The farmers were holding off planting, waiting for the much-needed rains. However, Buchan and his assistant Simeon were Christians and realized the window for planting was fast running out, so they decided to take action in faith. They reasoned that if they planted maize into the ground, despite how dry and dusty the ground was and how foolish it would appear to other farmers, God would answer their prayers and bring the necessary rains to make the seed grow and flourish.

So, in faith, they rolled out their tractors and the fertilizer, and planted the seed in dry ground believing God would answer their prayers and bring the much-needed rain. The ground was so dry that the dust rising from their tractors could be seen for miles around. However, despite what appeared to be foolish, they believed God had already answered their prayers as Mark 11:24 promises and planted the seed in dry ground despite what good farming practice told them. Read what happened in their own words:

> We all learned a valuable lesson from that crop. The Lord showed us the importance of walking by faith, and not by sight, of trusting him unconditionally and never giving up. At the end of the season we reaped five tonnes of seed per hectare. Most of the maize stalks had two cobs on them, and sometimes even three. It was the best crop I had ever harvested, and truly miraculous for a drought year. Farmers and friends came to look at the fields and gazed in amazement. All the praise and glory went to the supreme farmer, King Jesus. Everyone knew this could only have been a miracle (page 87).

They demonstrated their full assurance of faith in God that Hebrews 10:22 talks about by planting the seed and prayed God would bring the necessary rains. Operating and praying in faith, despite what the circumstances were dictating, brought the answer to prayer they needed. If they had simply stayed indoors without planting, nothing would have happened. But by going out and planting maize in the dry soil in faith, Buchan reaped the rewards which no other farmer did.

His planting was the outworking and evidence of his faith and trust in God.

He prayed and believed God had already answered. He didn't just sit back waiting for things to change first. His actions followed his faith even though he must have looked foolish to all the other farmers watching what he was doing.

As Hebrews 11 verse 1 teaches us, faith is the *substance* and *evidence* of what is not yet seen, and planting maize in dry ground is a great example of that. When we step out in faith, God meets us there. Although the situation looked completely impossible and crazy to do what they did, they exercised their faith in God and went ahead and planted. They trusted God's promises, not the circumstances around them. God loves that kind of faith, and it released His power.

It is never enough to just passively believe. The Biblical kind of faith that God looks for steps out, trusts God and has substance and evidence to it.

Bible miracle: Simon Peter walks on water

Simon Peter was one of Jesus' twelve disciples. He's known for being somewhat passionate, keen to please Jesus and often tried to go the extra mile to impress Him. When he saw Jesus Christ walking on the water, naturally he wanted to be a part of that too:

> "Shortly before dawn Jesus went out to them, walking on the lake. When the disciples saw him walking on the lake, they were terrified. 'It's a ghost,' they said, and cried out in fear. But Jesus immediately said to them: 'Take courage! It is I. Don't be afraid. 'Lord, if it's you, Peter replied, "tell me to come to you on the water.' 'Come,' he said. Then Peter got down out of the boat, walked on the water and came toward Jesus. But when he saw the wind, he was afraid and, beginning to sink, cried out, 'Lord, save me!' Immediately Jesus reached out his hand and caught him. 'You of little faith,' he said, 'why did you doubt?' And when they climbed into the boat, the wind died down. Then those who were in the boat worshipped him, saying, 'Truly you are the Son of God.'"
> Matthew 14:25–33

Simon Peter was the only disciple who had the courage and faith to join Jesus on the water. He invited himself to join Jesus, doing something completely miraculous. Jesus encouraged him and Simon Peter went for it. He walked over to the edge of that boat in full view of the other disciples, bunched up his clothing, swung his legs over the side of the boat and placed his feet on the water and walked towards Jesus. That was evidence of his faith in action.

Peter started to walk on the water. The other disciples must have stared at him in wonder. Things went well until he took his eyes off Jesus. He started looking around at the storm raging around him and fear began to fill his heart.

Fear is a real faith killer

Fear has a way of eradicating faith and so Peter started to sink into the water. Giving in to fear will always crush your faith in God. Whilst his confidence was in Jesus, he did the miraculous and walked on the water. However, the moment he took his eyes off Jesus and instead focused on the storm, he began to doubt and sink.

Don't allow the storms to quench your faith but protect your faith by reading God's Word, for His promises will strengthen and reinforce your faith. Focus on what God says and not on what the circumstances around you dictate. Remember, it's faith with substance that sees answers to prayer as Jesus taught in Mark 11:24.

Don't take your eyes off Jesus Christ and don't focus on the bad news you are hearing. Rather, lift your eyes and heart to God and put all your faith and hope in God your Father and His promises, to whom nothing is impossible. You will see the miraculous happen as you operate in faith.

Bible miracle: Jesus heals ten men with leprosy

Here is another great example of how moving in faith releases God's power:

> "Now on his way to Jerusalem, Jesus travelled along the border between Samaria and Galilee. As he was going into a village, ten men who had leprosy met him. They stood at a distance and called out in a loud voice, 'Jesus, Master, have pity on us!'
> Then he said them, he said, 'Go, show yourselves to the priests.' **And as they went, they were cleansed.**
> One of them, when he saw he was healed, came back, praising God in a loud voice. He threw himself at Jesus' feet and thanked him – and he was a Samaritan. Jesus asked, 'Were not all ten cleansed? Where are the other nine? Has no one returned to give praise to God except this foreigner? Then he said to him, 'Rise and go; your faith has made you well.'" Luke 17:11-19 (author's emphasis)

Jesus gave the ten men a command: to go and show themselves to the priests. There is no mention of Him praying over them, or commanding healing. They hadn't yet received their healing when He commanded them to embark on their trip to the priests. However, as they walked to the priests in faith, they received their healing.

I remember experiencing this principle one holiday. We had just landed in Australia after a long-haul flight when I became unwell. A few days before we left, I spoke at a Bible study for mothers and toddlers, and later that afternoon I found myself coming down with a sickness. I had recovered somewhat before leaving for the trip, but with jetlag and tiredness, it had reared its head again.

I spent the next few days in our rented apartment trying to recover. I took big doses of vitamin C and the usual counter medicines and rested, hoping I'd be better by the weekend. However, when the weekend arrived, I was worse. When Sunday rolled around, I'd had enough. This trip of a lifetime, with all the glorious sunshine teasing me outside, wasn't turning out as I expected.

That morning it dawned on me that even though I had been praying for healing, I hadn't backed up my prayers with any real substance or evidence of faith. In fact, I realized that I was doing was the very opposite: hiding in the apartment and taking medicine. If I really believed God had healed me, what was I doing? I repented for my lack of faith and started walking in faith, behaving as if I had already been healed.

I planned a full day of church and tourist activities. From the moment I started getting ready, I began to feel better. By the time I left the apartment an hour later, my head and sinuses had cleared, my sore throat had completely disappeared, my strength returned, and my faith had grown. We had a great day and rest of the week together.

I know it's just a trivial example, but it illustrates how there needs to be substance to our faith that makes it the kind of faith that Hebrews 11 talks about. When I eventually began to take steps of faith, my healing began. What we do by faith in the physical realm enables God's power to be released into our lives from the spiritual.

Bible miracle: Simon Peter heals a lame beggar

In this next miracle, we see Peter himself operating in faith for a miracle for a lame man. What is interesting is that this lame man didn't even ask for a miracle; he was begging for money. However, Peter knew he had something much more valuable he could provide and proceeds to perform a miracle for the man:

"One day Peter and John were going up to the temple at the time of prayer – at three in the afternoon. Now a man who was lame from birth was being carried to the temple gate called Beautiful, where he was put every day to beg from those going into the temple courts. When he saw Peter and John about to enter, he asked them for money. Peter looked straight at him, as did John. Then Peter said, 'Look at us! So that man gave them his attention, expecting to get something from them.
Then Peter said, 'Silver or gold I do not have, but what I do have I give you. In the name of Jesus Christ of Nazareth, walk.' **Taking him by the right hand, he helped him up, and instantly the man's feet and ankles became strong**. He jumped to his feet and began to walk. Then he went with them into the temple courts, walking and jumping, and praising God. When all the people saw him walking and praising God, they recognized him as the same man who used to sit begging at the temple gate called Beautiful, and they were filled with wonder and amazement at what had happened to him." Acts 3:1-10 (author's emphasis)

The act of faith in this story is where Peter took the lame man by the hand and pulled him to his feet. It's a big act of faith to pull a disabled person to their feet before you've seen any evidence of healing. However, as Peter operated in faith in the name of Jesus Christ, God's power was released, and the lame man was dramatically healed.

Whether it's the person in need who acts in faith or the person doing the praying, active faith releases God's power for miracles to meet our physical needs. There is nothing God cannot do in response to the prayer of faith in Christ's name. As Mark 1 teaches, we need to believe that God has answered, and *then* we will have our request.

> *Our faith must back up our prayers for it is the prayer of faith that is powerful and effective.*

All things are possible for those who believe.

Seek first God's kingdom and righteousness

Another important principle in James 5 to seeing answered prayer is also found in Matthew 6:25-34:

> "Therefore I tell you, do not worry about your life, what you will eat or drink, or about your body, what you will wear. Is not life more important that food, and the body more important than clothes? Look at the birds of the air; they do not sow or reap or store away in barns, and yet your heavenly Father feeds them. Are you now much more valuable than they? Can any one of you by worrying add a single hour to your life?
> "And why do you worry about clothes? See how the flowers of the field grow. They do not labour or spin. Yet I tell you that not even Solomon in all his splendour was dressed like one of these. If that is how God clothes the grass of the field, which is here today and tomorrow is thrown into the fire, will he not much more clothe you – you of little faith? So do not worry, saying, 'What shall we eat?' or 'What shall we drink?' or 'What shall we wear?' For the pagans run after all these things, and your heavenly Father knows that you need them. **But seek first his kingdom and his righteousness, and all these things will be given to you as well**. Therefore do not worry about tomorrow, for tomorrow will worry about itself. Each day has enough trouble of its own." (author's emphasis)

God promises that if we make His kingdom and righteousness a priority, giving thought to how we conduct our lives, He will take care of our practical necessities of life. We are made righteous before God through faith and the sacrifice of Jesus Christ:

"This righteousness is given through faith in Jesus Christ to all who believe." Romans 3:22

Righteousness is not something we can attain ourselves, nor something we can work for. A requirement of this saving faith of the gospel, however, is repentance and Jesus taught that we should produce fruit in keeping with repentance (Matthew 3:8). Repentance is basically changing your mind and going in a different direction. It's turning away from those habits and lifestyle that you know are displeasing to God. Repentance is important as there is no salvation without it.

Light and darkness cannot reside together. It matters how we live. We can't use God's grace as an excuse for living however we please. We can't walk in God's newness of life if we're still clinging on to our old way of life As James 5:16 says, it is the prayer of a *righteous person* that is powerful and effective.

If we take these words seriously, we don't need to worry about how our practical needs are going to get met because God promises to provide for us. If we busy ourselves in seeking first God's kingdom and His righteousness, He will busy Himself in providing for us. That doesn't mean we can become lazy and not work for the Bible teaches we should work (2 Thessalonians 3:10). Rather, it means He will do His part and provide for us as we do our part. He will provide that job, new home, clothing, food, healing or whatever we need as we seek His kingdom and righteousness first.

In the Lord's Prayer, Jesus invites us to ask God for our daily bread, representing the practical needs of life. As Philippians 4:19 promises, God will meet all our needs according to His riches in glory in Christ. God is a very practical God, and we can place our confidence in Him to do that as I have found time and time again.

Sofas

When God answers your prayers and meets your practical needs, those miracles stay with you. You never forget what God has done for you. After graduating from Bible College training, I took a full-time job and had just found my own place to live and I excited. It was a small house, and the lounge was L-shaped, so to maximise seating, I needed a 3-seater and a 2-seater sofa. I wanted leather sofas as I thought they would clean easy and last longer, and decided cream would be the best colour to compliment the room. Off I set around the various stores to find my sofas. However, I quickly learned that when you order a leather sofa in the UK, it takes around six weeks or longer to be made to order and I was moving into my new home in just two weeks' time.

There was one last furniture store to try. I had already spent a few days trying to find something, but without success. Options were running out. The salesman in that store did his best to find me what I needed, but it was clear that I wasn't going to be able to find what I needed in the time I needed them. What was I to do?

It was a large furniture store and I just sat there somewhat bewildered as to what to do, and to be honest, a little despondent. There was nowhere else to try. I prayed, "God show me what to do. Please provide!" I was out of options.

About ten minutes later, the salesman reappeared and came bounding towards me. "I'm glad you're still here. I've just got off the phone. A customer has just cancelled their order, and it's already here in the back storeroom. It's a cream 3-seater and 2-seater leather sofa. Do you want them?" I couldn't believe it! They were exactly what I was looking for and they had already been made and were ready in the back of the store waiting to be delivered. Those sofas lasted in that house around 20 years.

God taught me very clearly that as we seek His kingdom and righteousness first, we need never worry about our practical needs. Of course, that doesn't mean we have no responsibility. We need to do our part and as we do, God will do His. God wasn't going to float those sofas out of the sky to my front door. I needed to go out and look. These biblical principles really work!

Persevere in prayer

Another important principle we need to keep in mind when praying is the importance of perseverance seen in Luke 18:1-8 (NLT):

> One day Jesus told his disciples a story to show that should always pray and never give up. "There was a judge in a certain city," he said, "who neither feared God nor cared about people. A widow of that city came to him repeatedly saying, 'Give me justice in this dispute with my enemy.' The judge ignored her for a while, but finally he said to himself, 'I don't fear God or care about people, but this woman is driving me crazy. I'm going to see that she gets justice, because she is wearing me out with her constant requests!'
> Then the Lord said, 'Learn a lesson from the unjust judge. Even he rendered a just decision in the end. So don't you think that God will surely give justice to his chosen people who cry out to him day and night? Will he keep putting them off? I tell you, he will grant justice

to them quickly! But when the Son of Man returns, how many will he find on the earth who have faith?'"

Someone once asked me: how long should I keep praying? Until the answer comes. As Jesus taught, we should never stop asking when we bring our requests to God. God is just and will quickly bring about justice for His children. So if your answer is taking some time, don't give up. Keep praying until the answer comes just as Elijah did in James 5:17:

> "Elijah was a human being, even as we are. He prayed earnestly that it would not rain, and it did not rain on the land for three and a half years."

There had been no rain in the land for three and a half years. All the ponds and lakes dried up. No rivers or streams were flowing. Everyone was feeling it, including all the animals. God was trying to get people's attention. They had turned away in faith from God, largely influenced by King Ahab and his evil wife Jezebel. Elijah the prophet however, had done his best to turn people's hearts back to God and yet they were still unrepentant. Read what happened to Elijah in 1 Kings 18:1-2 and 41-46:

> "After a long time, in the third year, the word of the LORD came to Elijah, 'Go and present yourself to Ahab, and I will send rain on the land.' So Elijah went to present himself to Ahab."
>
> "And Elijah said to Ahab, 'Go, eat and drink, for there is the sound of a heavy rain.' So Ahab went off to eat and drink, but Elijah climbed to the top of Carmel, bent down to the ground and put his face between his knees. 'Go and look toward the sea,' he told his servant. And he went up and looked.

'There is nothing there,' he said.
Seven times Elijah said, 'Go back,'
The seventh time the servant reported, 'A cloud as small as a man's hand is rising from the sea.'
So Elijah said, "Go and tell Ahab, 'Hitch up your chariot and go down before the rain stops you.'
Meanwhile, the sky grew black with clouds, the winds rose, a heavy rain started falling and Ahab rode off to Jezreel. The power of the LORD came on Elijah and, tucking his cloak into his belt, he ran ahead of Ahab all the way to Jezreel." (author's emphasis)

Elijah prayed seven times and only stopped praying when he saw the first signs of rain coming. What is interesting in this Bible passage is that in verse 1, God told Elijah that He was going to send rain. Why did Elijah then need to pray for rain if God had already said He was going to send it?

As we have already looked at in the Lord's Prayer, we need to pray for God's kingdom to come and for His will to be done. We are in a spiritual battle and Satan is busy at work doing evil deeds, which are not God's will. So we need to pray for God's will to be done just as Elijah did here.

> *Sometimes God will show us His will about a matter, but we still need to pray it through*

Even though God had shown Elijah that He was going to send rain, Elijah still needed to pray for the rains to come. Seven times he told his servant to go and check for signs of rain. He didn't give up praying and he reaped the rewards.

Some answers to prayer come quickly, but then there are others that take longer. There are just some things take a bigger shift in the heavenly and earthly realms and need more prayer. Perhaps hearts need to change, circumstances need to be made ready, spiritual forces need to be pushed back, or it may just be a question of waiting for God's perfect timing. Whatever the reason, persevering in prayer for what you need is sometimes necessary.

Daniel and spiritual warfare

Perseverance in prayer can test and strengthen our faith and trust in God when it gets tough and we feel like giving up. Do we really trust God to answer? Perseverance can stretch our faith and deepen our trust in God. Other times we may need to persevere in prayer because there is spiritual warfare going on as was Daniel's experience, and we need to pray through that.

Daniel was a man of prayer who learned the importance of not giving up and why answers can sometimes be delayed. In Daniel 9, we see Daniel interceding for Israel. They had been taken into captivity seventy years earlier because of their persistent turning away from God. However, God had promised that after seventy years, He would bring them back to their homeland. Seventy years had passed and Daniel realising this, took God at His Word and prayed that God would fulfil His promise and bring His people back. The answer didn't come immediately and Daniel had to persevere in prayer. In Daniel 10:12-14 we learn why:

> "Do not be afraid, Daniel. Since the first day that you set your mind to gain understanding and to humble yourself before your God, your words were heard, and I have come in response to them. **But the prince of the Persian kingdom resisted me twenty-one days.** Then Michael, one of the chief princes, came to help me, because I was detained there with the king of Persia. Now I have come to explain to you what will happen to your people in the future, for the vision concerns a time yet to come." (author's emphasis)

This wasn't an earthly prince as you might expect, but an evil spiritual ruler over the geographical area of Persia. The angel who carried God's answer to Daniel's prayers was detained because he encountered resistance from spiritual forces of evil in the heavenly realms. Fortunately, another of God's angels, Michael, came to assist him and God's messenger was able to bring God's answer to Daniel. Sometimes, we just need to keep praying because the enemy is putting up a fight. Prayer is powerful and as you choose to persevere and not give up, the breakthrough will come.

Nothing is impossible for God. The prayer of a righteous person is powerful and effective. The prayer of faith can change the most impossible looking situation. Prayer is the most effective and valuable thing you can do for yourself and your loved ones. God can change any situation in response to your persevering prayers of faith. As you seek first God's kingdom and His righteousness, and pray and move in faith, placing your trust in the promises of God, you will see God do miraculous things in your life. God also promises to provide everything you need to do His work as 2 Corinthians 9:8 promises:

> "And God is able to bless you abundantly, so that in all things at all times, having all that you need, you will abound in every good work."

What a wonderful God we serve!

Prayer

Almighty God, you are the same God yesterday, today, and forever. You are the same God who has been miraculously providing for your people through the ages. God I pray You will provide for my daily needs. Help me to take you at Your Word and move in faith, knowing You will faithfully provide for me. Give me my daily bread I pray and help me always to persevere in prayer. In the name of Jesus Christ I pray, amen.

Questions for further study

1. How would you describe faith in your own words?

2. Why do you think faith is important when praying to God?

3. Out of the list of Bible promises mentioned in the chapter, choose one that is suitable for your needs right now. What scripture have you chosen and why?

4. Read Exodus 16:11-35. What did God provide for His people and for how long?

5. Read 1 Kings 17:7–24. What miracles do you see in this Bible passage?

6. What do you think would have happened to the widow if she hadn't followed Elijah's request?

7. Please read Matthew 21:18-22. What does Jesus teach about faith in these verses?

Chapter 7

And forgive us our debts, as we forgiven our debtors

Forgive us our debts [sins]

"When he [Jesus] had finished speaking, he said to Simon, 'Put out into deep water, and let down the nets for a catch.' Simon answered, 'Master, we've worked hard all night and haven't caught anything. But because you say so, I will let down the nets.
When they had done so, they caught such a large number of fish that their nets began to break. So they signalled their partners in the other boat to come and help them, and they came and filled both boats so full that they began to sink.
When Simon Peter saw this, he fell at Jesus' knees and said, 'Go away from me, Lord; I am a sinful man!' For he and all his companions were astonished at the catch of fish they had taken, and so were James and John, the sons of Zebedee, Simon's partners.
Then Jesus said to Simon, 'Don't be afraid; from now on you will fish for people.' So they pulled their boats up on shore, left everything and followed him." Luke 5:4-11

Encountering the grace and power of God transforms our lives and sends us in a completely new and positive direction, one that we were never expecting. I'm sure Simon Peter that day never expected to encounter the Christ, nor have his sins forgiven, nor be invited to a new purpose in life. But that is what happened to him when he met Christ and in time, he became a powerful preacher and the leader of the Early Church. He is not the only one whose life has dramatically changed. All around the world today there are many who are encountering the love, grace and power of Jesus Christ, being transformed and finding God's purpose for their lives as a result.

God's grace and forgiveness are powerful. We all have a past. We've all said or done things we regret, wishing we could turn back time and undo. But we can't. They're there engrained in our history, the consequences of which we live with. However, God can completely forgive all those things and give us a brand-new start, wiping our slate clean. The Bible says, when God forgives us, He remembers our sins no more and our sins are washed away. Hallelujah!

Forgiveness from God is important for several very important reasons: to have our sins dealt with and be reconciled to God, to be saved from hell and receive the promise of eternal life, find healing, and to have peace in our own hearts and minds.

But why do we need forgiveness at all? In Exodus 20, God gave the Ten Commandments: do not steal, murder, or commit adultery. Do not give false witness about your neighbour or covet his possessions or spouse. Not worship any other god or idol but worship the LORD our God only, and not use His name incorrectly. We should keep the Sabbath day of rest and honour our parents. These commandments reveal God's will about how we should live our lives.

I personally don't know anyone who has never transgressed God's commandments. Do you? I transgressed God's commandments even as a child. There are many wonderful people around the world who are very kind and caring, doing good deeds to help others in need, but who are not immune from sin and transgress God's commandments. Even the best of people sin from time to time.

This tendency towards wrongdoing is engrained in our nature. When God first created humankind, He created us perfect and without sin. We were not made with this inclination, but later the first man and woman, Adam and Eve, chose to disobey God's one and only command at the time, the consequences of which introduced evil to the world. As God said would happen, their eyes were opened to good and evil, and sin and death came into the world. It's been everyone's struggle and experience ever since.

What they did not only caused a breach in their relationship with God, but had lasting negative consequences for themselves starting with being expelled from the Garden of Eden where they had once enjoyed sweet fellowship with their Maker. Sin always causes a breakdown in relationship. If someone sins against you, it damages the relationship. Unless there is genuine repentance and forgiveness, the relationship can't be restored to what it once was.

It's the same with our relationship with God. When we sin we breach our relationship with Him, and there needs to be genuine repentance. We need to ask Him to forgive us our debt of sin. However, as with any debt, there is a cost to it being paid off. Debts need accounting for. There is always a cost to sin. However, God knew we couldn't pay our own debts, so God stepped in for us and sent His Son, Jesus Christ, to come to earth and pay for our debts, by dying on a cross in our place, for our sins:

> "He himself bore our sins in his body on the cross, so that we might die to sins and live for righteousness." 1 Peter 2:24

Jesus Christ has paid for your debts and mine, providing the way for our debt to be satisfied, forgiven and restored before God. Therefore when we confess our sins to God, He is faithful to forgive us because of what Jesus Christ has done for us, just as 1 John 1:9 promises:

> "If we confess our sins, he is faithful and just and will forgive us our sins and purify us from all unrighteousness."

As we repent of our sins and confess our sins to God, we are forgiven and our relationship with God is restored and life truly begins as the following parables from the Bible show.

The woman caught in adultery

This story in the Bible from John 8:2-11 gives us a real glimpse into the loving and gracious heart of God:

> "At dawn he [Jesus] appeared again in the temple courts, where all the people gathered around him, and he sat down to teach them. The teachers of the law and the Pharisees brought in a woman caught in adultery. They made her stand before the group and said to Jesus, 'Teacher, this woman was caught in the act of adultery. In the Law Moses commanded us to stone such women. Now what do you say?' They were using this question as a trap, in order to have a basis for accusing him.
> But Jesus bent down and started to write on the ground with his finger. When they kept on questioning him, he straightened up and said to them, 'Let any one of you

who is without sin be the first to throw a stone at her. Again he stooped down and wrote on the ground.

At this, those who heard began to go away one at a time, the older ones first, until only Jesus was left, with the woman still standing there. Jesus straightened up and asked her, 'Woman, where are they? Has no one condemned you?'

'No one sir,' she said.

'Then neither do I condemn you,' Jesus declared. 'Go now and leave your life of sin.'"

We can be so quick to condemn the obvious sin in other people's lives without paying any attention to our own sin. We quickly point the finger to others, all the while ignoring the sins in our own lives hidden from others. We can be such hypocrites just like these religious people in the story. They were ready to throw stones and condemn this woman, but Jesus didn't. Instead, He gave her grace, forgiveness and direction for her future. Grace will powerfully pull us towards God, showing us the heart of God, lovingly inviting us to walk in His ways. God is always ready to forgive the repentant heart. As God says in Matthew 9:13, "But go and learn what this means: 'I desire mercy, not sacrifice.' For I have not come to call the righteous, but sinners." God loves us and is ready to forgive us the moment we come to Him in repentance and faith.

The Prodigal Son

It's never too late to come back to God, no matter where you've been or what you've done. God your heavenly Father waits for His children to return as Jesus Christ explained in the following parable:

Jesus continued, "There was a man who had two sons. The younger one said to his father, 'Father, give me my share of the estate'. So he divided his property between them.

Not long after that, the younger son got together all he had, set off for a distant country and there squandered his wealth in wild living. After he had spent everything, there was a severe famine in that whole country, and he began to be in need. So he went and hired himself out to a citizen of that country, who sent him to his fields to feed pigs. He longed to fill his stomach with the pods that the pigs were eating but no one gave him anything. When he came to his senses, he said, 'How many of my father's hired servants have food to spare, and here I am starving to death! I will set out and go back to my father and say to him: Father, I have sinned against heaven and against you. I am no longer worthy to be called your son; make me like one of your hired servants'. So he got up and went to his father.

"But while he was still a long way off, his father saw him and was filled with compassion for him; he ran to his son, threw his arms around him and kissed him.

"The son said to him, 'Father, I have sinned against heaven and against you. I am no longer worthy to be called your son.'

"But the father said to his servants, 'Quick! Bring the best robe and put it on him. Put a ring on his finger and sandals on his feet. Bring the fattened calf and kill it. Let's have a feast and celebrate. For this son of mine was dead and is alive again; he was lost and is found.' So they began to celebrate. " Luke 15:11-24

The father in this story gave no telling off or rebuke when his errant child came home, just love, forgiveness and acceptance. When he spotted his son on the horizon, he literally ran to meet him. The father was so delighted to have his son back, that he threw his arms around his beloved child and kissed him. The welcome didn't stop there. He swapped his son's dirty rags for the best robe and put on a feast to celebrate his return. He put a ring on his finger symbolising identity and belonging. This son who had squandered everything his father had once given him, was completely reinstated as a son, dearly loved by his father.

When Jesus Christ told parables, they always had an important meaning, and this parable's meaning is clear: God is overjoyed when we return to him. He is a generous Father, exchanging our rags for a righteous robe, giving us a new identity and a place in His family. We are so loved.

Zacchaeus the Tax collector

Let's look at one more story in the Bible where Jesus was ready to show love and grace to someone who others were ready to reject:

> "Jesus entered Jericho and was passing through. A man was there by the name of Zacchaeus; he was a chief tax collector and was wealthy. He wanted to see who Jesus was, but because he was short he could not see over the crowd. So he ran ahead and climbed a sycamore-fig tree to see him, since Jesus was coming that way.
> When Jesus reached the spot, he looked up and said to him, 'Zacchaeus, come down immediately. I must stay at your house today.' So he came down at once and welcomed him gladly.
> All the people saw this and began to mutter, 'He has gone to be the guest of a sinner.' But Zacchaeus stood up and said to the Lord, 'Look, Lord! Here and now I give half of my possessions to the poor, and if I have

cheated anybody out of anything, I will pay back four times the amount.'
Jesus said to him, 'Today salvation has come to this house, because this man, too, is a son of Abraham. For the Son of Man came to seek and save the lost." Luke 19:1-10.

Tax collectors in Jesus' day were notorious for overcharging customers and extorting money from people. They didn't have a good reputation, which is why the crowd were describing Zacchaeus as a sinner. Those watching were ready to condemn him, yet Jesus knew his heart, that he was ready to repent and change his life. Zacchaeus was hoping to get just a glimpse of Jesus, yet Jesus invites Himself to his house. Can you imagine how thrilled and honoured Zacchaeus must have felt?

Jesus is always ready to forgive the one whom others are ready to condemn. Jesus came to seek and save the lost. We just need to come to Him in repentance and faith, and salvation and a changed life will follow. Jesus Christ has already paid the punishment you and I deserve in full. You don't need to beat yourself up or live in guilt. That's not God's will for you for as Isaiah 53:10 (ESV) teaches, Christ's death was not only a sin offering but a guilt offering too. In other words, God wants to wipe away your sins and your guilt. He wants to give you a fresh start and remembers your sins no more. As these parables show, God is so good, kind and merciful and He loves you. Don't hesitate to come to Him and ask Him for His forgiveness in Christ.

As we forgive our debtors [those who sin against us]

We've looked at putting right our debts of sin before God, but there are other debts that might need squaring away in our lives: those that others have committed against us.

For many of us, this will be the hardest section of the Lord's Prayer because we've all had people who've hurt us and let us down, and whom we struggle to forgive. However, choosing to not forgive someone and instead hold on to grudges and hurt can do us harm. In Mark 11:24,25, Jesus taught one very important fact when it comes to prayer and learning to forgive:

> "Therefore I tell you, whatever you ask for in prayer, believe that you have received it, and it will be yours. And when you stand praying, if you hold anything against anyone, forgive them, so that your Father in heaven may forgive you your sins."

God commands us to forgive others because He has forgiven us. He has cleared our debt before Him; we should therefore be willing to clear the debt of others. Choosing to forgive those who've hurt you is one of the best things you can do for yourself for several reasons.

Benefits of forgiving others

Firstly, if we choose to forgive others, then God will forgive us. However, if we choose to withhold forgiveness, Jesus taught that God the Father will withhold forgiveness *to us* as Mark 11 implies. In the Lord's Prayer, Jesus repeated this fact:

> "For if you forgive other people when they sin against you, your heavenly Father will also forgive you. But if you do not forgive others their sins, your Father will not forgive your sins." Matthew 6:14-15.

Given the fact that God has forgiven us for so much sin, God asks us to forgive the sins of others against us. It's more than an obligation; it's a command of God. When we forgive someone who has wronged us, it's not that we're saying what they did was OK. Not at all. That's not what forgiving others is about. Withholding forgiveness affects our relationship with God and also causes *us* problems. If we don't forgive, it opens the door to bitterness, resentment and anger, and these attitudes can cause us difficulties. Jesus taught a parable, which highlights the importance of forgiving others in Matthew 18:21-35:

> "Then Peter [a disciple of Christ] came to Jesus and asked, 'Lord, how many times shall I forgive my brother or sister who sins against me? Up to seven times?'
> Jesus answered, 'I tell you, not seven times, but seventy-seven times.
> Therefore, the kingdom of heaven is like a king who wanted to settle accounts with his servants. As he began the settlement, a man who owed him ten thousand bags of gold was brought to him. Since he was not able to pay, the master ordered that he and his wife and his children and all that he had be sold to repay the debt.
> At this the servant fell on his knees before him. 'Be patient with me,' he begged, 'and I will pay back everything,' The servant's master took pity on him, cancelled the debt and let him go.
> But when that servant went out, he found one of his fellow servants who owed him a hundred silver coins. He grabbed him and began to choke him. 'Pay back what you owe me!' he demanded.
> His fellow servant fell to his knees and begged him, 'Be patient with me, and I will pay it back.'
> But he refused. Instead, he went off and had the man thrown into prison until he could pay the debt. When the other servants saw what had happened, they were outraged and went and told their master everything that had happened.

Then the master called the servant in. 'You wicked servant,' he said, 'I cancelled all that debt of yours because you begged me to. Shouldn't you have had mercy on your fellow servant just as I had on you?' In anger his master handed him over to the jailers to be tortured, until he should pay back all he owed.
This is how my heavenly Father will treat each of you unless you forgive your brother or sister from your heart.'"

This is a serious warning. Whether you think you are like the man who owed ten thousand bags of gold or a hundred silver coins, Jesus' point is we need to forgive as God has forgiven us our debt of sin. How will you respond to those who have hurt you and done you wrong? Unforgiveness robs from you. I've seen people live with offence for decades. It has slowly destroyed their relationship with God, their involvement with Church and His purpose for their lives. Unforgiveness also steals our peace. There is nothing good about withholding forgiveness and does us no good whatsoever. Like I said, it's not saying that what they did to you was OK. Rather, it's about setting yourself free from what they did to you and obeying God your Father. God will deal with them for what they did to you.

Some may blame God for the wrongs that others have done to them. What we need to remember is when others sin against us, they're also sinning against God. It's not at all God's will when people harm and abuse others. It grieves God too and God will deal with them. Evil deeds are the work of our adversary, the Devil. He is out to destroy us and our faith in God, and unforgiveness is one of his most effective tools towards that goal. Evil is always close by where unforgiveness exists.

A second benefit of choosing to forgive someone is God can then deal with that wrong that was done against you. If you're still holding on and dealing with it in your own way, you're not allowing God to deal with it. Instead, surrender the wrong into His hands. Say to God, 'Lord, I trust you to deal with that person and the wrong they did to me. I trust you to give me justice. Please heal me.' It is His job to avenge you, not yours:

> "Do not repay anyone evil for evil. Be careful to do what is right in the eyes of everyone. If it is possible, as far as it depends on you, live at peace with everyone. Do not take revenge, my dear friends, **but leave room for God's wrath, for it is written, 'It is mine to avenge; I will repay,'** says the Lord. On the contrary: 'If your enemy is hungry, feed him; if he is thirsty, give him something to drink. In doing this, you will heap burning coals on his head.' Do not be overcome by evil, but overcome evil with good." Romans 12:19-21 (author's emphasis)

God will do a far better job of dealing with that wrong and the person who did that to you than you will. Give Him room to do that as Romans 12 says and give room to God in your heart and forgive them, and be set free.

The third benefit of forgiving others is because carrying unforgiveness in our hearts leaves a door open for our enemy, Satan, to use. Unforgiveness often resides with its acquaintances: anger, resentment, hatred, bitterness, aggression, and vengeance. These attitudes are very harmful to our soul and lead to all sorts of other negative side effects we might not realise: insomnia, nightmares, depression, anxiety, even physical ailments. It opens a door for evil spirits to torment us, the torturers that Jesus spoke of in the parable above. We cannot separate our soul from our physical body for what goes on in our soul will impact our bodies. If you are living with resentment and unforgiveness, it will at some point impact you mentally or physically or both. However, as we choose to forgive, we close the door to the enemy and are set free from these harmful effects. When you forgive, God is then able to bring healing into your life. Forgiving others will set you free from the negative influences of the enemy and will give you peace in your heart where you didn't have it before. When we forgive, we let go of the offence into God's hands and that thorn can no longer causes us pain and anger in our hearts. *Only then* can God heal the pain and damage the person caused whether physical, emotional or mental.

I remember on one occasion, a new colleague in a church I was working at said something to me that hurt. He didn't know me really as he'd only been there a few months but I felt judged and misunderstood. As the weeks went by, I realised that resentment was growing in my heart and I needed to forgive him. With God's help, I repented of my attitude towards him and forgave him. However, I still felt hurt in my heart and so I asked God to take away the pain. As soon as I did, I literally felt the pain leave! God removed it. I was so overjoyed by what God had done, I couldn't stop smiling in our next meeting. However I know that if I hadn't forgiven him, I would never have received God's healing because I would have remained in disobedience to God's command to forgive. But once I forgave him, God answered my prayer and the healing followed. God is so good.

Don't allow unforgiveness to fester and turn into hatred for hatred is akin to murder in God's eyes and can potentially impact our eternal destination:

> "Anyone who hates his brother is a murderer, and you know that no murderer has eternal life in him." 1 John 3:15.

Choose to forgive and you will see the blessings of God released into your life. The person may not know that you will have forgiven them but God knows and you too will know the real benefit of extending that grace. Even Jesus Christ chose to forgive those who put Him on the cross. Whilst hanging on the cross, Jesus prayed:

> "Father, forgive them, for they do not know what they are doing." Luke 23:34

It is of no benefit to you holding on to wrongs. Quite the opposite. As you make the decision to forgive, God will forgive you, heal you and He will deal with the wrong. You will then be able to move on. Forgive, and you will see God's blessings flow to you.

As the words of the Lord's Prayer teach us, we only have a right to ask God to forgive us as we forgive others. It's the best thing we can do for ourselves. Release that hurt and pain to God and entrust it to Him to deal with and avenge. Forgive those who've hurt and abused you, who've taken advantage of you, mistreated you or spoken ill of you. Forgive just as God has forgiven you. Maybe that person who wronged you hasn't apologised or tried to put it right. Maybe they haven't repented and are still harassing you. God will deal with them and will rescue you. You do your job and God will do His.

Don't worry about any fallout from what happened to you. God has got your back. He will take care of you and is able to fulfil His purpose in your life despite what others may have said or done. If someone stole from you, God could provide for you again. Ask God to heal the scars, whatever kind they are. There is nothing God cannot heal or provide for. But it all begins with your decision to obey God and forgive.

Forgiveness may be a process for some of us and we may need to remind ourselves on a number of occasions that we have forgiven that person. Ask God to help you and give you the heart to forgive and move on, and He will. Over time, it will get easier and it will be worth it.

Forgiving abusers

For those who've experienced abuse at the hands of others, forgiving someone does *not* mean that you have to reconcile that relationship. There may be some relationships where God does ask that of you, but it will certainly not be the case every time. God does not want anyone to place themselves in danger from being harmed by evil or abusive people. The Bible teaches us to stay away from people who do evil, so use wisdom and protect yourself. You can forgive from a distance. Not all relationships should be restored.

This is also not about getting the other person to repent. That's not your job. Whether that person is alive or has passed away, repented or not, it is necessary to go through that process of forgiveness between you and God for your benefit, to set you free so you can be healed, forgiven, and move on.

If there is someone whom God has brought to mind as you've been reading this chapter that you need to forgive, choose today to deal with that offence. Don't carry it any longer but allow God to set you free. Give it to God and bless yourself. Carrying unforgiveness towards them is doing you more harm than it's doing them. God wants to set you free from that burden and its tormentors. Move forward into God's freedom and healing. You may wish to use the following prayer to begin that process:

Heavenly Father, you know the wrongs that _____ [name] did against me. What they did has hurt me deeply. Lord, because you ask me to, I choose today to forgive _____ for the wrong they have done against me. I forgive them for everything

they've said and done. I entrust this wrong into your hands and I ask you to deal with them and avenge me and bring me justice. Please also heal me of the damage it has done in my life - body, mind and soul. I give the wrong to you to deal with and I ask you to heal my life completely. Please restore my life Father God, and give me your peace, filling me with your Holy Spirit. In the name of Jesus Christ I pray, amen.

Final word

If you'd like to read more on this subject of learning how to forgive others, I recommend the excellent book, *Bait of Satan*, by pastor and author John Bevere.

Isaiah 61:3 teaches us what God can do with our brokenness:

> "[T]o comfort all who mourn, and provide for those who grieve in Zion – to bestow on them a crown of beauty instead of ashes, the oil of joy instead of mourning, and a garment of praise instead of a spirit of despair. They will be called oaks of righteousness, a planting of the LORD for the display of his splendour."

God change turn our ashes into something beautiful. God is in the transformation business. He can exchange our mourning for joy and our despair for praise. He can take the years of abuse or harm and heal us deeply, transforming our lives into something beautiful. So attractive, your life will become a display of God's splendour. It's God's speciality. It doesn't matter what you have experienced in the past. God is all about making our lives brand new. God can give you a wonderful new start and a future as Jeremiah 29:11-14 says,

"For I know the plans I have for you," declares the LORD, "plans to prosper you and not to harm you, plans to give you hope and a future. Then you will call on me and come and pray to me, and I will listen to you. You will seek me and find me when you seek me with all your heart. I will be found by you," declares the LORD, "and I will bring you back from captivity."

God wants to transform your life and bless you with hope and a future. Whatever you past, you have a wonderful future with God.

Questions for further study

1. Read Isaiah 53. Who do you think this chapter is talking about?

2. What did this person do according to verses 5, 6, 11 and 12?

3. According to verse 9, did this man deserve this punishment?

4. Read verse 10. What kind of offering was his life? What do you think that means for you?

5. Now read Psalm 103:1-5. What are some of the many benefits of being a child of God?

6. Compare Psalm 103:3 and Isaiah 53:4. What common theme do these verses have?

7. What is one benefit of choosing to forgive someone in your own words?

Chapter 8

And do not lead us into temptation, but deliver us from the evil one

When we pray these words of the Lord's Prayer, do we comprehend what we're praying? I know I didn't for many years. What does it mean to be delivered from the evil one? Delivered from what exactly?

If we take a moment to consider what some people we know may be going through, we see all kinds of problems. From physical infirmity or mental ill-health to fears and crippling addictions, personal struggles are part of our human experience. Many are battling something. The causes are also many from generational problems being passed down, being the victim of an unfortunate accident, to consequences of a harmful habit or the negative influence of others.

For some reason, God often gets the rap for the problems we encounter. We rarely point the finger to the Devil. Yet from what we read in the Bible, he's the author of evil and suffering that we're so familiar with. As Jesus said, the Devil comes to steal, kill and destroy but Jesus came to bring life. So why do we blame God if we're experiencing the handiwork of Satan?

We need God's intervention in our lives, bringing healing and freedom, and this chapter is all about how we can experience that. How we be set free from all kinds of negative and destructive problems we face, which Jesus described as the works of the evil one. Jesus considered this need so important for us, He included it in His prayer. So let's take some time to learn how we can apply Christ's victory in our own lives.

Do not lead us into temptation

Many of us are all tempted by something in life that, if indulged, will not do us any good. Then there are other temptations that can lead into real harm. It's so hard to resist temptation when we're in the thick of it, so Jesus taught us to pray and ask God to protect us from being drawn into it in the first place. We need to pray for our own protection.

Let's clarify something here: temptation itself isn't sin. It's only when we give in to it that it leads down that path. Even Jesus Himself experienced temptation as Hebrews 4:15-16 explains:

> "For we do not have a high priest who is unable to empathize with our weaknesses, but we have one who has been tempted in every way, just as we are – yet he did not sin. Let us then approach God's throne of grace with confidence, so that we may receive mercy and find grace to help us in our time of need."

These verses teach us that we can experience temptation and still not sin. That was Jesus' experience. He knows what it's like to be tempted in every way, just as we are, and yet He didn't give in. Because He's been there, He empathizes with us. These verses encourage us to turn to and approach God for help when we're feeling the fires of temptation. They're the very moments we need to draw near to God for help and not turn away in shame or embarrassment. Jesus identifies with our struggles and is compassionate towards us in our fight. In such moments, we are invited to turn to God and His throne of grace and as we do, we will find the help we need to overcome. We do not need to face and battle temptations alone. God is there beside us, full of grace and love, to strengthen and help us walk into victory.

If we do find ourselves drawn into the power of temptation, it's still not too late as God promises He will provide a way out for us:

> "No temptation has seized you except what is common to man. And God is faithful; He will not let you be tempted beyond what you can bear. But when you are tempted, he will also provide a way out so that you can stand up under it." 1 Corinthians 10:13.

God will not allow us to be tempted beyond what we can cope with. He will always provide us with a way out. Of course, it's our choice whether we take that way out or not. If someone has a problem with alcohol and prays that God would help them not be led into temptation, and then decides to go for a walk down to the local bar, that is not taking God's way out of temptation. That's putting your head in the lion's mouth and expecting it to not bite you. God is there to provide a way out of temptation, but we have to make the decision to take it.

For 40 long days in a hot and weary desert, Jesus endured testing and temptation prior to the launch of His ministry. How hard those days must have been, not forgetting that He fasted during it all too:

> "Then Jesus was led by the Spirit into the wilderness to be tempted by the Devil. After fasting forty days and forty nights, he was hungry. The tempter came to him and said, 'If you are the Son of God, tell these stones to

become bread.' Jesus answered, 'It is written: 'Man shall not live on bread alone, but on every word that comes from the mouth of God.'" Matthew 4:1-4.

The Devil tried three times to tempt Jesus, but each time, Jesus responded with firm resistance and the Word of God. Temptation only leads to sin when we give in to it. Say no and walk away. The Devil works hard to tempt and entice us but we are encouraged to look for God's way out and take it:

"When tempted, no-one should say, 'God is tempting me.' For God cannot be tempted by evil, nor does he tempt anyone; but each one is tempted when, by *his own* evil desire, he is dragged away and enticed. Then, after desire has conceived, it gives birth to sin; and sin, when it is full-grown, gives birth to death." James 1:13-15 (author's emphasis)

It's only when our desire has conceived it leads into sin. The key to successfully resisting the temptations of the Devil is found in James 4:7:

"Submit yourselves, then, to God. Resist the Devil, and he will flee from you."

Resisting begins with submitting ourselves to God and His will for our lives, with a surrendered heart willing to obey Him. If we're not, we will find it very hard to resist temptation. Submit to God, trust in Him, resist the Devil and you will experience God's victory. Pray for your own protection from temptation, that you would not be led into it. Pray that for your loved ones too.

PART B

Deliver us from the evil one

Next Jesus taught us that we need to pray God will deliver us from the evil one, Satan, also known as the Devil. Both names mean the same: accuser or slanderer.[7] One thing we need to understand: the Devil is *not* an equal adversary to God. Not by any stretch. For sure, he has his kingdom here on earth and is wreaking havoc in all forms. However, God is far greater and more powerful and is working to defeat the evil deeds of the enemy, healing the damage to people's lives.

Before he fell, Satan was a created being, a high-ranking angel serving God before pride and ambition got hold of his heart.[8] Read what Jesus said to His disciples about Satan's downfall in Luke 10:18-20 and the power in Christ we have over him:

> "He [Jesus] replied, 'I saw Satan fall like lightning from heaven. I have given you authority to trample on snakes and scorpions and to overcome all the power of the enemy; nothing will harm you. However, do not rejoice that the spirits submit to you, but rejoice that your names are written in heaven.'"

God has given us the authority and power to overcome all the power of the enemy. This is possible because when Christ died on the cross and rose from the dead three days later, He conquered the power of sin and death and all the power of the Satan (Colossians 2:13-15) as we looked at in in chapter four.

---

[7] Satan is his Hebrew name from the Old Testament and Devil is his Greek name from the New.

[8] Isaiah 14:12-14 and Ezekiel 28:12-18.

> *When Christ died on the cross and rose from the dead three days later, He conquered the power of sin and death and all the power of the evil one.*

Although Satan may still be at work for now, we are called to pray and apply God's kingdom power and victory over evil. It's so important that we pray and ask God to do that. In response to our prayers, God can heal and undo any damage the enemy has done. There is no pain and suffering God cannot heal and restore. This what Jesus spent so much of His time doing when He walked on this earth, fulfilling His mission by bringing freedom and healing as He stated in Luke 4:18-21:

> "'The Spirit of the Lord is on me, because he has anointed me to proclaim good news to the poor. He has sent me to **proclaim freedom for the prisoners and recovery of sight for the blind, to set the oppressed free**, to proclaim the year of the Lord's favour." Then he [Jesus] rolled up the scroll, gave it back to the attendant and sat down. The eyes of everyone in the synagogue were fastened on him. He began by saying to them, 'Today this scripture is fulfilled in your hearing.'" (author's emphasis)

God is ultimately sovereign, and Christ's victory can be brought and applied into any situation to defeat Satan's work. Let's take a closer look at some of the areas in our lives that the enemy often tries to work and how we can overcome them in Christ.

Your thought life

One of the Devil's greatest tactics, which many don't realise, is to plant negative thoughts in our minds that are not our own. This happens much more than we realise. Negative or tempting thoughts about our identity, value, weaknesses, and our future often originate from the enemy of our souls. Do any of the following sound familiar:

> You're no good; you might as well give up
> No one cares about you
> You're useless; you have no future
> You're not in the right body
> You're different to everyone else
> You're not normal
> You'll never be able to change
> God doesn't love you

Lies, lies and more lies. Satan loves to plant suggestions in our minds that are just *not true*. Jesus made it clear Satan is the father of lies and an accuser of God's people. We should not listen to or accept what he says.

I remember when I first became a Christian at the age of seventeen, whenever I tried to pray, I'd have blasphemous thoughts suddenly come to mind. It was quite disturbing and at first I didn't understand what was going on. I had no church background and was brand new to the faith, so I didn't know anything at the time about spiritual warfare. But as I began to read the Bible and grow in God, I realised the Devil was trying to stop me from praying. To try to combat this, I decided I would praise God out loud every time it happened, and so that is what I did. The plan worked. The blasphemous thoughts soon stopped.

I remember another occasion, many years later, Satan tried to convince me something about my identity. He put an ungodly thought in my mind that I knew from Scripture was not God's will, and I thought to myself, no, that's not who I am. That's not true nor what I want to do. I rejected the suggestion of the evil one and found myself declaring out loud that I loved righteousness. As I did, I literally felt an evil spirit flee my presence! That was another valuable lesson to me that day on how the Devil works, and where unrighteous and negative thoughts often originate from.

Don't believe or accept every thought that enters your mind. They're not all your own.

Many people don't understand what is going on in the battlefield of the mind and accept all thoughts as being theirs. As a result, we either accept these thoughts and submit to them thinking they're our own, or reject them but dwell in guilt or shame. Don't listen to the Liar! Discern the temptations of the enemy and understand what is going on. As James 4:7 promises, submit to God, resist the Devil and he will flee. Remember, temptation itself isn't sin.

The Devil will try to get us to doubt our identity in God. This is nothing new as he even tried to get Jesus to doubt His identity as the Son of God (Matthew 4). However, Jesus knew who He was and resisted the Devil, refusing to give in to his requests. We need to do the same.

The Devil does not want you to prosper. Nor does he want you to discover God's will and purpose for your life. If he can convince you of a lie and mess your life up, he absolutely will. Resist him and reject his lies. Following God's plan for your life begins by surrendering to God's will as we've seen. Once you've done that, resisting the evil one becomes easier and Satan will flee from you because he's a defeated foe:

> "Be self-controlled and alert. Your enemy the Devil prowls around like a roaring lion looking for someone to devour. Resist him, standing firm in the faith."
> 1 Peter 5:8-9

If you are having trouble with negative or dark thoughts, instead of trying to push those thoughts out of your mind, which can be exhausting work, choose to think about something positive instead. Switch track. It's much more effective. For example, read what the Bible says about you and your identity. Fill your heart and mind with the truth of God's Word. Transformation happens by the renewal of our minds (Romans 12:2). Leaning on God's Word is essential if you're going to overcome the lies of the enemy just as Jesus did when He was tested and tempted. We need to do the same.

Here are some helpful examples of true and positive thoughts from the Bible that you may find helpful:

> I am a child of God – John 1:12
> I am a friend of Jesus Christ – John 15:15
> I have been bought with a price and I belong to God – 1 Corinthians 6: 19 - 20
> I have been chosen by God and adopted as His child – Ephesians 1: 3 – 8
> I am complete in Christ – Colossians 2:9 - 10
> I am free from condemnation – Romans 8:1 – 2
> Nothing can separate me from God's love – Romans 8:31 – 39
> I have not been given a spirit of fear but of power, love and a sound mind – 2 Timothy 1:17
> I am God's workmanship – Ephesians 2:10
> I can do all things through Christ who strengthens me – Philippians 4:13
> I am born of God and the evil one cannot touch me – 1 John 5:18
> I have been established, anointed and sealed by God – 2 Corinthians 1:21 – 22
> I have direct access to God's throne of grace through Christ – Hebrews 4: 14 – 16

These are wonderful truths of Scripture, true for you. Every time a negative thought comes to mind, declare a truth of God and praise God out loud. The Devil hates that and will soon give up as you resist. Pray therefore that God would lead you away from temptation and that He would deliver you from the evil one. Surrender to God and don't give in to the Satan's schemes:

> "Anyone you forgive, I also forgive. And what I have forgiven – if there was anything to forgive – I have forgiven in the sight of Christ for your sake, in order that Satan might not outwit us. For we are not unaware of *his schemes.*" 2 Corinthians 2:11 (author's emphasis)

Satan is a schemer and will use anything to make us fall and pull us away from God and His wonderful purpose for our lives. Typical schemes he uses include an ex-partner who doesn't know God suddenly reappearing in your life, an old friend suddenly reconnecting who has a negative influence, a new partner on the scene who has no interest in living according to God's ways, or someone who has hurt you in the past reappearing and stealing your peace and joy. I've seen it numerous times in people's lives. Satan is pretty apt at creating circumstances to tempt and lure a person away from God.

The last thing the Devil wants is for you to enter into God's great plans for your life. However, Jesus came to give you life and life to the full. God has a wonderful future for you, which is far better than anything you can imagine, so don't let the enemy lure you away from God through one of his schemes. Look for God's way out and pray God would deliver you from the evil one so that you can fulfil God's amazing plan for your life as Jeremiah 29:11 promises. God is ready and able to lead you into victory if you are submitted to Him and willing.

PART B

Spiritual oppression

Another wicked scheme of the enemy is to oppress and afflict people in some way, making their lives a misery. Much of the work Jesus Christ, by contrast, revolved around setting people free, bringing much needed healing or deliverance into their lives:

> "Jesus went throughout Galilee, teaching in their synagogues, proclaiming the good news of the kingdom, and healing every disease and sickness among the people. News about him spread all over Syria, and people brought to him all who were ill with various diseases, those suffering severe pain, the demon-possessed, those having seizures, and the paralyzed; and he healed them. Large crowds from Galilee, the Decapolis, Jerusalem, Judea and the region across the Jordan followed him."
> Matthew 4:23-25

Jesus Christ encountered many people who were either afflicted with physical sicknesses, oppressed from unclean spirits, or both, and He healed and delivered everyone who came to Him.

It is not God's will for people to live life tormented and sick.

Jesus came to give us life to the full and to bring healing into people's lives, setting them free from the works of the evil one. Nothing has changed. The same problems Jesus encountered still exist today with many people still in need of healing and freedom from physical sickness or spiritual oppression and torment. God continues to set people free.

Recognise spiritual problems

There's so much talk today in our cultures about mental ill health, which takes various forms including depression, anxiety, and self-harming to bipolar, schizophrenia and suicidal tendencies. These ailments are prevalent in our society, but they're not a recent phenomenon. It's only now social media provides a platform for people to talk about them openly. Sadly, there's a real lack of understanding of these problems in many churches today. There is no need to be hesitant or embarrassed about having conversations about these kinds of problems.

Whilst no doubt, some of these conditions originate from physical causes such as chemical imbalances in the body, more often than not, they're the result of spiritual problems. It's quite easy to spot spiritual affliction in someone's life. Symptoms of potential spiritual problems at work include:

- Depression
- Nightmares
- Overwhelming fear and anxiety
- Voices in one's head
- Mental blocks
- Suicidal tendencies
- Hopelessness
- Rejection and abandonment
- Spirit guides
- Unexplained scratches on one's body
- Hallucinations
- Fears and phobias
- Various addictions
- Self-harming
- Paranoia
- Physical sickness
- Anger and rebellion

- Blasphemous thoughts

If you are suffering from any of these, be filled with hope and expectation for God can completely heal and transform your life. The Bible clearly teaches that this is God's will because He loves you and cares deeply for you. No one need stay in their suffering. Jesus Christ came to heal us and set us free. You can experience complete healing and freedom from whatever afflicts you.[9]

Causes of spiritual affliction

Before I begin to explain some of the causes of affliction, I want to state a most important fact: *Christ has given His followers the power and authority to heal and set people free from all kinds of spiritual and physical sicknesses and affliction.* Please keep that in mind as we go through the next section. If you think you might be suffering from some kind of affliction or sickness, we will look in the next chapter how God can heal you and set you free.

Behind some forms of fear, depression and oppression are unclean spirits at work, afflicting people, making their lives a misery, and hindering the good plans God has for them. Spiritual harassment can happen to the most genuine of Christians and the loveliest of people. Satan is happy to oppress anyone.

> *Whatever the type of spiritual oppression and whatever the cause, there is always a reason.*

We need to understand that there is always a reason why someone is suffering the way they are, which must

---

[9] There are supportive ministries such as Sozo and Ellel Ministries who specialise in healing and deliverance prayer and ministry. You can visit one of their centres if you need further support.

be addressed and healed if someone is going to experience complete freedom. Let's consider some of the most common reasons for affliction.

- *Spiritual attack* – Over the years, I have noticed that if someone is growing in God or bearing fruit for His Kingdom, Satan will try to stop them. I recall a spiritual attack I experienced when I was in my early thirties and about to change career and enter into full time pastoral ministry. I was coming to the end of my teaching job and had just finished my lectures for the day. It was early afternoon and a warm and glorious sunny day. As I got into my car to drive home and set my papers on the passenger seat, suddenly there was a very loud scraping noise all over my car. It sounded like there was something sat on top of it scraping each side: left and right, then front, back and again, moving all very fast. It lasted about ten seconds. I just sat in the driver's seat stunned. There was no one around and no human was strong or fast enough to able to do what I was hearing. I realised it was a spiritual attack. I knew God was greater so I just laughed it off and prayed that God would help me drive home safely. I believe Satan tried to instil fear into me that day, to deter me from switching into ministry, but his scheme didn't work.

In another example years later, I had just planted a church in South Wales that previous year. We rented a community hall for our services each Sunday and it was just a fifteen-minute drive there from my house. I recall how during the drive to church every Sunday, a depression would settle on me out of nowhere to discourage me. It was subtle but after a few months of this happening, I realised what was really going on. To combat this this spiritual warfare, I decided I would pray in tongues. Sure enough, after a few Sundays of doing this, the depression never came back.

- *Sickness* – this is one of the enemy's biggest weapons against God's people, using some kind of sickness to try and prevent people from living the full life Jesus promised. I will explain more on this later in this chapter.
- *Ungodly influences* – this is another way we make ourselves vulnerable to spiritual problems, through social media and entertainment on our screens. The internet and media are full of ungodly content: computer games centred on fighting and killing, and films, books and music on horror, murder, magic, sexual immorality, dissension, and godlessness. Fortune telling, magic, and spirit guides are also available anytime and anywhere through our phones. Our children are being taught that magic is fun and adventurous, fighting and murder is normal, and sexual immorality is something to be admired and experimented with. Do we really think that what we watch on our screens is not going to affect and influence us? No wonder people suffer from so much affliction. These are ungodly and evil influences and when we engage in them, we open ourselves to the influence of unclean spirits. These influences are harming our children and youth too and it's time we woke up to this.
- *Footholds* – Another very common reason is because the enemy has gained a small foothold in our lives. This can happen in numerous ways and can often be entirely no fault of our own, or at other times, through our own sin. Examples of the former include being the victim of a negative experience such as physical or sexual abuse, which can open a door to fear, depression, or even suicidal thoughts intruding in your life. Other negative experiences include having a bad accident such

as a road traffic accident or a serious fall. These can lead to fear and anxiety. Being abandoned can lead to rejection or depression. I'm not saying these outcomes always happen, but they *can* happen depending on the vulnerability and response of the person.
- *Sin* - A further cause behind spiritual oppression or affliction is the result of our own sin, lifestyle and activities we've engaged in, providing a foothold from which Satan can cause us further problems. Let's take a closer look.

Sin gives the Devil a foothold

The Bible clearly teaches us that how we conduct ourselves can lead to giving the Devil a foothold in our lives:

> "Therefore each of you must put off falsehood and speak truthfully to your neighbour, for we are all members of one body. 'In your anger do not sin'. Do not let the sun go down while you are still angry, and *do not give the Devil a foothold.* Anyone who has been stealing must steal no longer, but must work, doing something useful with their own hands, that they may have something to share with those in need." Ephesians 4:25-28 (italics added)

Engaging in sin gives the Devil a foothold in our lives, from which he can cause us problems. A foothold is an area of our life from which he can operate to oppress and trouble us. There are always consequences to sinful actions or words. When Adam and Eve sinned in the Garden of Eden (Genesis 3), their sin gave the Devil authority to come into the world, bringing evil and its close allies: death, sickness, pain, and suffering. Sin gives the enemy a legal right and authority to work and oppress us. No matter how long you have been a Christian, if you are continuing to sin in an area, it will hold you back from growing in God and will give a foothold to the Devil in your life. You will need to repent and renounce that sin, closing the door to the enemy and surrendering that area back to God.

Sin gives Satan a foothold in our lives

Some are still struggling with issues in their lives because they have not repented of a particular sin, giving the enemy the right to retain that area of their lives to operate from, as it's not surrendered to God. How we live matters to God. We can't just hide under the blanket of God's love and grace and think how we conduct ourselves and treat others is of no effect. That is not what the Bible teaches. We give the enemy a foothold in our lives through ongoing sins such as gossip, lying, slanderous accusations, blasphemy, condemnation, manipulation, corruption, rage, violence, deception, witchcraft, Ouija boards, tarot cards, spirit worship, horoscopes, spiritualism, shamanism, other religions, selfish ambition, stealing, bribery, unforgiveness, sexual immorality, pornography, addiction, laziness, idleness, and other sins. Through these, we give the Devil a place in our lives and churches where he can do his destructive work, and we play right into his hands. This is often how unclean spirits have a right to afflict us.

Let's be clear: Christian or not, sin gives Satan a foothold in our lives. It gives him the right and authority to work, and if a foothold isn't dealt with and we fall deeper into sin, it can grow and develop into a stronghold in our lives.

The good news is God is still in the life changing business, and He wants you and I to enjoy the fullness of life He promised. He doesn't want anyone to live with oppression, depression or sickness. Jesus came to set us free. When Jesus walked the earth, He healed countless people from all sorts of problems: physical, spiritual, and mental. Jesus is still doing His kingdom work today.

If you think sin may be the cause of problems you are experiencing and you want to be set free, turn from that sin. Your words *and* actions must reflect that change. Mere talk isn't enough. Throw away any objects that are connected to that sin (for example digital content, phone apps, books, tarot cards, alcohol and so on). You may even need to bring an end to a relationship if it is leading you away from God. God will help you and give you the strength to obey Him and He will bless you for it. When we repent, we are taking back that ground from Satan, and surrendering it back to God's authority and protection, cutting off the right to the enemy. In addition to repenting, you may also need prayer to evict an unclean spirit. Unless they are evicted and commanded to leave in the name of Jesus Christ, they will continue to cause us problems, Christian or not.

When deliverance is needed

Now that we've looked at some of the reasons behind the spiritual affliction and torment that people suffer, I just want to pause here and talk about deliverance as there is a lack of understanding about the subject. Often when we think of deliverance, we may think of what we've seen in movies: someone being completely taken over or some other outlandish phenomena going on. No wonder some are afraid to broach the subject if this is our point of reference.

Movies do *not* accurately portray deliverance ministry. Deliverance is simply commanding an evil spirit in the name of Jesus Christ to stop afflicting someone and leave that person's life. That's it. It is nothing to be at all afraid of or embarrassed about. I've gone through deliverance myself and the freedom that follows is so worth it.

Some Christians seem appalled by the suggestion that there may be an evil spirit afflicting them, as if it implies that the person is evil or under judgement. However, as I've just explained, there are many ways we can be oppressed and troubled by an unclean spirit. The best of Christians can suffer this way.

Spiritual oppression versus spiritual possession

We need to clearly distinguish between oppression and possession. There is a difference. Possession describes someone like the man at Gerasenes in the story below whom Jesus delivered. Such a person's life is so dominated by an evil spirit (or multiple spirits), they can be described as possessed. They do not function well in society and are often not able to take care of themselves as the spirits have significant influence. This man was tormented mentally and spiritually and his case particularly acute. He self-harmed, lived alone and would cry out from his affliction and torment:

> "They went across the lake to the region of the Gerasenes. When Jesus got out of the boat, a man with an impure spirit came from the tombs to meet him. This man lived in the tombs, and no one could bind him anymore, not even with a chain. For he had often been chained hand and foot, but he tore the chains apart and broke the irons on his feet. No one was strong enough to subdue him. Night and day among the tombs and in the hills he would cry out and cut himself with stones.
> When he saw Jesus from a distance, he ran and fell on his knees in front of him. He shouted at the top of his voice, 'What do you want with me, Jesus, Son of the Most High God? For Jesus had said to him, 'Come out of this man, you impure spirit!' Then Jesus asked him, 'What is

> your name?' 'My name is Legion,' he replied, 'for we are many.' And he begged Jesus again and again not to send them out of the area.
> A large herd of pigs was feeding on the nearby hillside. The demons begged Jesus, 'Send us among the pigs; allow us to go into them.' He gave them permission, and the impure spirits came out and went into the pigs. The herd, about two thousand in number, rushed down the steep bank into the lake and were drowned." Mark 5:1-13

If this man were alive today, he would probably be diagnosed with a serious mental health condition, medicated, and locked up in a mental health ward. As the case for many such patients, that would not be dealing with the real cause of his affliction through deliverance and healing, but just managing the symptoms. Jesus crossed that lake to that region specifically to set that man permanently free:

> "When they came to Jesus, they saw the man who had been possessed by the legion of demons, sitting there, dressed and in his right mind; and they were afraid…
> As Jesus was getting into the boat, the man who had been demon-possessed begged to go with him. Jesus did not let him, but said, 'Go home to your own people and tell them how much the Lord has done for you, and how he has had mercy on you.' So the man went away and began to tell in the Decapolis how much Jesus had done for him. And all the people were amazed." Mark 5:15 and 18-20

Oppression, however, is when someone's life is afflicted by an evil spirit, but they can carry on as normal whilst trying to cope with the sickness it brings. This is quite different. There are plenty of people who are suffering under some kind of affliction caused by evil spirits, often through no fault of their own, and are still able to function in life and take care of themselves. Even so, an unclean spirit has somehow latched on causing that person to suffer in some way, making life difficult. It's the difference between having an unwanted back seat passenger in your car and someone upfront behind the wheel. The woman in Luke 13 had an unwelcome evil spirit afflicting her until Jesus set her free:

> "On a Sabbath Jesus was teaching in one of the synagogues, and a woman was there who had been crippled by a spirit for eighteen years. She was bent over and could not straighten up at all. When Jesus saw her, he called her forward and said to her, 'Woman, you are set free from your infirmity.' Then he put his hands on her, and immediately she straightened up and praised God. Indignant because Jesus had healed on the Sabbath, the synagogue leader said to the people, 'There are six days for work. So come and be healed on those days, not on the Sabbath.'
> The Lord answered him, 'You hypocrites! Doesn't each of you on the Sabbath untie your ox or donkey from the stall and lead it out to give it water? Then should not this woman, a daughter of Abraham, whom Satan has kept bound for eighteen long years, be set free on the Sabbath day from what bound her? When he said this, all his opponents were humiliated, but the people were delighted with all the wonderful things he was doing." Luke 13:10-17

What is worth noting in this passage is that Jesus calls this woman a daughter of Abraham. In other words, a woman of genuine faith. This passage clearly shows that a beloved follower of God can still suffer from oppression by an evil spirit manifest through physical affliction. Here was a woman who loved God, worshipped in a synagogue service, and yet was suffering from a spirit of infirmity which had crippled her for eighteen long years. Jesus places His hands on this daughter of God, and she is delivered from the spirit of infirmity and healed physically as a result.

Christians who are filled with the Holy Spirit can absolutely be troubled by an unclean spirit they may not have yet recognised or dealt with. We all came to faith at some point in our lives, and may not have yet addressed the issues we developed prior to knowing God. When we are saved and come to know God, all our issues are not automatically sorted and healed straight away. Some may be, but oftentimes, there are still problems from the past we need to address and seek God for understanding and healing on. There are a lot of Christians who live life with unaddressed problems that need God's touch. If we don't address them, these issues remain with us and can cause us ongoing spiritual or physical problems.

Spiritual oppression then is not the same as demonic *possession*. Rather, it's harassment by the enemy, manifested physically, mentally or spiritually, enough to make our lives hard to bear, whatever the cause. Possession only happens when we allow a foothold of the enemy in our lives to become a stronghold, which if still unaddressed over the years, can lead to degrees of control over our lives.

God is far more powerful than any affliction and is ready to set anyone free when they turn to Him. Unclean spirits tremble before the name of Jesus Christ. Rebuking and commanding an unclean spirit to leave is recommended for anyone who suffers from any level of affliction by the enemy. Please do not be afraid or hesitant about pursuing freedom if you have an issue in your life you cannot control or get victory over. The first step will require addressing the reason the problem exists in the first place. Inner healing or repentance may be needed and God can help you with that, setting you free and ushering in the healing Jesus came to give us all. You don't have to continue living in your suffering. Freedom is absolutely possible in Christ. Whether you need physical healing or spiritual deliverance, or both, God can set you free from whatever afflicts you. Don't let fear, pride or embarrassment hold you back. I will explain how you can be set free in the next section of this book.

Testimony of mental healing: Ann

A friend whom I'll call Ann has been suffering from schizophrenia for almost three decades. She hears voices regularly and has really suffered from her condition over the years, spending time in a mental health hospital early on. It has been impossible to engage in conversation with Ann as she would often appear distracted, with her gaze fixed elsewhere in the room listening to the voices in her head.

For many years, I just didn't understand her illness and didn't know how to pray for her. I knew she had smoked Cannabis as a young adult at university and that she had engaged in Shamanism and other new age practices, which I came to realise probably opened the door to the enemy to afflict her. I eventually came to believe that despite the severity of her affliction, God was indeed able to heal her. However, because she hadn't yet chosen to follow God and was still interested in fortune telling, she wasn't ready for full deliverance. So, I just prayed that God would bring healing into her life.

After about a year of praying for her on and off, God brought about a tremendous change. She is now able to have conversations and look at people in the eye like anyone else, which she couldn't do previously. You wouldn't know she was unwell other than she still does hear voices. Deliverance prayer would sort that. I've told her this, but until she has surrendered her life to Christ and repents of the reasons she became unwell in the first place, it's not recommended as the spirits would probably come back (Matthew 12:43-45). She engages in conversation now and doesn't switch off anymore. On one occasion, she told me she can't understand how she got healed, so I explained how God had simply answered prayer. She is slowly understanding more about God, and I pray that one day she'll be ready for the final stage of freedom through deliverance.

Through Ann's healing, I've seen first-hand how God can bring healing to someone with a serious mental health condition. There is no one God cannot heal and restore to health.

Physical sicknesses caused by evil spirits

Let's look a bit more now at how some physical sicknesses have a spiritual problem as its cause. Jesus understood this and would know when just physical healing was needed or something more:

> "Then they brought him a demon-possessed man who was blind and mute, and Jesus healed him, so that he could both talk and see." Matthew 12:22-23

Sometimes when someone was brought to Jesus with a physical problem, He performed deliverance from an unclean spirit and they were physically healed as a result as we saw with the woman in Luke 13. The Bible clearly teaches that some physical sicknesses are caused by evil spirits.

Some physical illnesses have a spiritual problem at its root

I'm certainly not saying that all physical illnesses are caused by spiritual oppression, but a good number do have a spiritual problem at its root. I have seen numerous times when someone is walking well with God, the enemy will try to put a stop to that by oppressing them in some way, usually either physically or practically. As we looked at in chapter two, Ephesians 6 makes it very clear that we are in a spiritual battle but that we can overcome the Devil's schemes with the weapons God has provided for us. Whatever you're facing, there is no need to give in to fear or hopelessness for you can experience victory through Jesus Christ.

Physical problems that may have a spiritual cause include *some* (not all) types of cancer, deafness, blindness, infertility, arthritis, seizures, physical deformity, growths, unexplained physical sicknesses and pain, and more. Like I said, I'm *not* saying that is the cause in every case, but in some circumstances, it's worth exploring. Let us look at a few more scriptures where we see a physical ailment with oppression from an evil spirit at its root:

> "When the spirit saw Jesus, it immediately threw the boy into a convulsion. He fell to the ground and rolled around, foaming at the mouth.
> Jesus asked the boy's father, 'How long has he been like this?'
> 'From childhood,' he answered. 'It has often thrown him into fire or water to kill him. But if you can do anything, take pity on us and help us.'
> 'If you can?' said Jesus. 'Everything is possible for one who believes.'
> Immediately the boy's father exclaimed, 'I do believe; help me overcome my unbelief!'
> When Jesus saw that a crowd was running to the scene, he rebuked the impure spirit. 'You deaf and mute spirit,' he said, 'I command you, come out of him and never enter him again.'
> The spirit shrieked, convulsed him violently and came out. The boy looked so much like a corpse that many

said, 'He's dead.' But Jesus took him by the hand and lifted him to his feet, and he stood up." Mark 9:20-27

"God anointed Jesus of Nazareth with the Holy Spirit and power, and how he went around doing good and healing all who were under the power of the Devil, because God was with him." Acts 10:38

Clearly there are problems that might have a physical manifestation but the root cause is spiritual. Jesus placed great emphasis not only on physical healing but deliverance too. Even children can suffer from oppression from unclean spirits, something that is more prevalent than we realise. Violence, aggression, hatred, and communication problems in children and young people may have a spiritual problem behind them. Think about what our children are exposed to today. Is it any surprise this is the case? Trauma or violence in the home, bullying at school, engaging in violent computer games and TV programmes, magic, all provide footholds to the enemy. Spiritual problems can also be passed down through a parent or grandparent. The young boy in our story was deaf and mute, and suffered from seizures, but the root cause was an unclean spirit, which Jesus rebuked and commanded to leave, bringing complete healing. God is so good and desires to set everyone free, whatever our age or situation.

We have looked at in this chapter what it means when Jesus taught to pray that we would not be led into temptation, and that God would deliver us from the evil one. Because Jesus Christ has defeated the power of Satan through His death and resurrection, He can set us free from whatever afflicts us, whether it has a physical cause or spiritual. If you think that your problem may have a spiritual root, the next section will show you how to deal with that, once and for all, finding victory in Christ.

PART B

Questions for further study

1. Do you struggle in believing negative thoughts about yourself? If yes, what does the truth of God's Word say about that?

2. What have you learned about temptation from this chapter? How does God help us overcome?

3. Is there an unexplained physical or spiritual affliction that you are suffering from? If yes, what is that?

4. Do you think it might have a spiritual root problem?

5. Do you think you may have given the enemy a foothold in your life? If yes, what do you think that was? Have you dealt with that before God previously, or does it still need dealing with?

6. How would you explain the difference between spiritual oppression and spiritual possession in your own words?

7. Is there a generational problem in your family that you think might need addressing in prayer?

Part C

Pray for healing and deliverance

Chapter 9

How to pray for healing

"Heal me, O Lord, and I shall be healed; save me, and I shall be saved, for you are my praise." Jeremiah 17:14

Praying for healing from sickness should be a common practice among believers in Christ as this is God's revealed will in scripture. If someone is sick, they can pray in faith in the name of Jesus Christ for it is God's will to heal any type of sickness as my husband Anthony experienced:

> The tiredness started when I was thirteen years old. I caught glandular fever and for some people, there are long term side effects. I had the fever for months and months and was eventually taken to the doctor who discovered I had an enzyme deficiency. By the time I was seventeen, I had developed chronic fatigue. Much of the time, I couldn't get out of bed as I just didn't have the energy. I would also have to crawl up the stairs in my home.
> The fatigue would come and go. Some days I would be fine, others I would feel wrecked. Spending time in the sun seemed to help, feeling like I had more energy. I used to actively seek out the sun and therefore hated winters because the sun wasn't strong enough, and nights,

because it made me feel depressed. Another side effect was I was constantly bitten by insects. On one camping trip to Scotland, I had thirty insect bites on each arm. It was so bad, I packed up in the middle of the night and went home. This was how my life was until I was in my early thirties.

One day I was prayed for by a friend in a house church, who anointed my head with oil. From that point on, everything changed. I didn't suffer from the chronic fatigue anymore. God's healing has made a big difference in my life. I am so thankful to God for His healing. Even insects don't come near me anymore.

We can pursue healing from God in several ways: you can either pray for healing for yourself, attend a healing meeting to receive prayer from a speaker offering healing, or you can ask a leader of our church to pray for healing for you:

"Is anyone among you in trouble? Let them pray. Is anyone happy? Let them sing songs of praise. Is anyone among you sick? Let them call the elders of the church to pray over them and anoint them with oil in the name of the Lord. And the prayer offered in faith will make the sick person well; the Lord will raise them up. If they have sinned, they will be forgiven. Therefore confess your sins to each other and pray for each other so that you may be healed. The prayer of a righteous person is powerful and effective." James 5:13-16

There have been many servants of God through the centuries, both men and women, whom God has used to bring healing and deliverance to many thousands of people in need. John G. Lake, Kathryn Kuhlman, Smith Wigglesworth, St. Patrick, and Charles and Frances Hunter are just a few of the many people who have been greatly used by God. Through the ministry of John G. Lake (1870 – 1935), over 100,000 people were recorded as healed in a five-to-six-year period in his healing rooms in Spokane, Washington. Many more were healed through his healing crusades in various countries. In his healing rooms, the sick would come and stay, leaving their medication at home. They would have scriptures read to them each day to build up their faith in confidence in God's promises, and then receive prayer for healing. This 'treatment' would help them understand that it is God's will to heal, strengthen their faith, and as a result, many left his rooms miraculously healed.

More recently we are blessed by the ministries of Randy Clark, Heidi Baker, Carlos Annacondia, Robby Dawkins, Bill Johnson and many more who are not so well known. God is still in the healing business and all around the world, people are receiving miraculous healings and deliverances in the powerful name of Jesus Christ. The ministry of healing is not just for those who have healing gifts and make it a full-time profession. *All believers* in Christ are invited to pray for healing in the name of Jesus Christ. That includes you. God our Father heals anyone who calls on Him in faith through His Son Jesus Christ because it is He who has made healing available.

Jesus Christ: Healer and Freedom Giver

Healing is possible for us because of Jesus Christ. So much of what Jesus did when He walked this earth revolved around healing the sick and setting the oppressed free, as well His teaching on many important subjects:

> "The scroll of the prophet Isaiah was handed to him. Unrolling it, he [Jesus] found the place where it is written: 'The Spirit of the Lord is on me, because he has anointed me to proclaim good news to the poor. He has sent me to

proclaim freedom for the prisoners and recovery of sight for the blind, to set the oppressed free, to proclaim the year of the Lord's favour.' Then he rolled up the scroll, gave it back to the attendant and sat down. The eyes of everyone in the synagogue were fastened on him. He began by saying to them, 'Today this Scripture is fulfilled in your hearing.'" Luke 4:17-21

Jesus Christ came to be our wonderful Saviour, but He also came to heal the sick and set us free from the destructive works of the evil one, doing the good works the Father showed Him.

There is no sickness or oppression God cannot heal

Anyone who turns to Him in genuine humility and faith can experience His love and healing power. God is still setting people free from physical and spiritual problems including:

- all kinds of physical sickness and disabilities no matter how hopeless or terminal
- debilitating allergies
- creative miracles (restoring or regrowing missing body parts)
- addictions
- gripping fears (anxiety, nightmares, claustrophobia, crowds, public spaces, panic attacks, fear of death)
- mental health problems including anxiety, depression, schizophrenia, and bipolar
- demonic oppression
- unforgiveness, hatred, anger, and bitterness

This list is not exhaustive. God can undo and completely restore any work that Satan, the enemy of our souls, has wreaked in our lives. I have experienced firsthand the blessing of receiving God's healing in my own life and the lives of friends and family.

Healing from ongoing dizziness

When I was in my mid 30s, I lived in a studio apartment which had polished wooden stairs leading to the bedroom. One day as I was coming down these stairs, I slipped and fell down about half a dozen steps, landing on the side of my head. Thankfully I happened to land on a rug that was at the foot of the stairs, but nonetheless, I was still badly concussed. I couldn't get up and sat on the floor for several hours before being able to slowly wiggle myself a few feet to phone for help. I nursed a black eye for a few weeks. However, what really affected me was whenever I lay down to go to sleep at night, the room would spin. Every night this would happen. I hoped it would eventually stop, but the opposite happened. After a few months, it got worse and started happening in the mornings too when I got up.

I went to the hospital for a scan, but they couldn't find any cause for the dizziness, so I figured it was time to seek healing from God. That Sunday after service, I explained to my church small group what had happened and asked them to pray for healing for me. They simply prayed that God would heal me of the dizziness and God answered. I was immediately healed, and I've never experienced it since. My small group shared my joy when I told them the following Sunday how God had healed me in answer to their prayers. I am so grateful to God for His healing touch.

Healing from heart palpitations

My job as an associate pastor in Seoul was a busy one indeed. South Koreans have a strong work ethic and working long hours is the norm. There was a period of six months or so whilst working as a pastor where I developed very bad heart palpitations every night when I tried to sleep. They were getting worse as the months went by and started to frighten me. I decided to visit my doctor who did some tests and confirmed I had a heart disorder no doubt related to the long hours I worked. He advised he could prescribe tablets to help me feel less stressed if I wanted them, but I refused and decided I would take the matter to God in prayer instead.

I prayed and asked God to heal me of the night heart palpitations. God answered my prayers and they immediately stopped. I was so grateful to God for His healing touch.

Healing from serious food allergy

In my pastoral work, a church member, Sunny, told me how she had been feeling suicidal because of a severe eating allergy she had. She had suffered from it for years and it caused her significant physical pain and misery and was robbing her of her joy. There were many foods she couldn't eat, and she suffered physically whenever she ate something by accident. She was very disheartened, but I encouraged her to believe that God could and would heal her. I knew of a healing conference that was coming up in another church where a well-known healing evangelist was speaking at, and I strongly encouraged her to attend.

It took a bit of persuading but eventually, she went. She said the minute she walked into the conference room, she knew God had healed her. No one had yet prayed for her, but she knew God had touched her body. She went home and in great faith, ate food that she knew she previously couldn't eat, and confirmed her healing. This healing transformed her life and before long she was making new career plans for herself.

Healing from a blood disorder

My husband recalls a time when he prayed for one of his students and God healed her:

> When I was teaching in my adult IT classes, I would offer prayer to my students during the break times for anything. On one occasion, a student shared that she had recently been diagnosed with a blood disorder by her doctor. She used to get very tired and was worried as she didn't know what that meant for her future, and asked if I would pray for her. She didn't know God personally but was keen to receive prayer. Together with one of her friends, I prayed that God would heal her, commanding the sickness to leave in the name of Jesus Christ.
>
> A few weeks later she had gone for more tests but was told that the disorder had completely gone, and her energy had returned. Praise God for His wonderful healing power.

The Bible teaches it is God's will to heal

As all these testimonies attest, the Bible teaches it is God's will to heal today. There are numerous Bible verses that encourage us to have faith and ask and believe God for what may seem impossible in our lives:

> "Very truly I tell you, **whoever believes in me [Jesus] will do the works I have been doing, and they will do even greater things than these,** because I am going to the Father. And I will do whatever you ask in my name, so that the Father may be glorified in the Son. You may ask me for anything in my name, and I will do it." John 14:12-14 (author's emphasis)

What a tremendous promise! Jesus said that anyone who believes in Him will do the wonderful works He had been doing. Even greater things in fact! This promise is relevant for you and I today. God always keeps His promises. We just need to know how to walk in them.

As we ask God for what we need and see God answer, it not only blesses the person receiving the healing, but it brings glory to God too. When people see a divine healing, it creates faith in God and draws people to Him. Healing then brings numerous positive outcomes as well as meeting the need of the person who received the answer: God is praised, our faith is strengthened, our relationship with God is deepened, our prayer lives are invigorated, others are encouraged to pray for healing for themselves, and it draws not-yet believers to God in saving faith. Seeking God and receiving answers to our prayers is a wonderful blessing for all these reasons.

We have already looked at the commission Christ gave His church prior to His ascension in Mark 16:15-18 (ESV):

> "And he said to them, 'Go into all the world and proclaim the gospel to the whole creation. Whoever believes and is baptised will be saved, but whoever does not believe will be condemned. And these signs will accompany those who believe: in my name they will cast out demons; they will speak in new tongues; they will pick up serpents with their hands; and if they drink any deadly poison, it will not hurt them; they will lay their hands on the sick, and they recover.'"

Healing the sick and setting free the oppressed are all part of the Great Commission Christ has entrusted to us. We have been commissioned to continue His work. Jesus said, 'whoever believes' in Him will do the things He did and even greater works. We have been entrusted to take

His good news message to a hurting world, praying for the sick and setting free the oppressed. Jesus also said that we would do even greater things because He was leaving earth to return to the Father, essentially handing over the baton to His Church. Given the fact that Jesus healed so many and even raised the dead, I struggle to imagine what He meant by 'greater things', but it must be awesome!

Healing is for everyone

There is no indication in the Bible that God limits healing, that it is His will to heal some and not others. Quite the opposite for Jesus healed everyone who came to Him:

> "When evening came, many who were demon-possessed were brought to him, and he drove out the spirits with a word and **healed all the sick**. This was to fulfil what was spoken through the prophet Isaiah: 'He took up our infirmities and bore our diseases.'" Matthew 8:16-17 (author's emphasis)

This is such as interesting passage as the quote mentioned from Isaiah 53, talks about Christ's death and resurrection and the purpose of it all: to die for our sins and guilt *and* heal us from our sicknesses. Matthew 8 specifically links Christ's work of healing the sick to fulfilment of the Isaiah 53 prophecy, which says:

> "Surely he hath borne our griefs [sicknesses], and carried our sorrows [pains]" (Isaiah 53:4 KJV with footnotes)

What Christ accomplished on the cross brought about even more than we realise:

Christ died for our sins and our sicknesses

"With his stripes we are healed." (Isaiah 53:5 KJV)

Think about what these verses are saying: the blood of Christ was shed for the forgiveness of our sins *and* our healing. Both were made possible through what Christ accomplished on the cross. God wants to make us completely whole. The Bible clearly teaches that it is God's will to forgive us of our sins *and* heal us from our infirmities, diseases, and pains. *Both were made possible through the death and resurrection of Christ.* That's what Matthew 8 and Isaiah 53 are talking about. You can be confident of God's will to heal because Christ has already made it possible.

Sometimes, receiving forgiveness and physical healing are connected. That is, we need to forgive before we receive God's healing. God desires to touch every area of our lives. There is no need to limit what God can do because He is wonderful, loving, merciful and is in the life transformation business. He always keeps His promises. However, for some healing does not come straight away. If that's the case, there is usually a reason behind it. One should not just give up hope for healing at that point. Instead, we need to seek God and consider whether there is an area of our life that needs God's touch and intervention. Let's take a look at some common 'blockages'.

Dealing with blockages

There's one fundamental thing you need to realize about God: He is very good, and He loves you and wants the best for you. Often a person will experience healing immediately. However, for others, their healing is delayed. There can be various reasons for that:

- The need to forgive someone or receive forgiveness
- Healing of an inner wound

- Mistaken thinking about yourself or God
- A curse that needs to be broken
- Our faith and trust in God needs to be strengthened

These kinds of issues can temporarily block our physical healing, but once dealt with, the healing will flow. I've encountered instances in ministry when a person came forward for prayer to receive physical healing, but God revealed a completely different issue that needed addressing first. The fact is, sometimes we need more than physical healing, which God knows. As you seek Him in prayer for physical healing, don't be surprised if God highlights another important area of your life He wishes to bring peace and healing into first. As issues or blockages are dealt with, the physical healing will follow.

The need to be forgiven

One issue could be an area of sin that hasn't been dealt with yet. Sin can block God's healing power from flowing into our lives and God may want to address that first as persistent sin can prevent us from growing in God and continue to cause us all kinds of problems. There are consequences to sin including guilt, self-loathing, sickness, damaged relationships, financial bankruptcy, or addiction to name a few. In the following Bible passage, a man was brought to Jesus for physical healing but Jesus addressed the issue of forgiveness first:

> Some men came, bringing to him a paralyzed man, carried by four of them. Since they could not get him to Jesus because of the crowd, they made an opening in the roof above Jesus by digging through it and then lowered the mat the man was lying on. When Jesus saw

their faith, he said to the paralyzed man, "Son, your sins are forgiven."
Now some teachers of the law were sitting there, thinking to themselves, "Why does this fellow talk like that? He's blaspheming! Who can forgive sins but God alone?"
Immediately Jesus knew in his spirit that this was what they were thinking in their hearts, and he said to them, "Why are you thinking these things? Which is easier: to say to this paralyzed man, 'Your sins are forgiven,' or to say, 'Get up, take your mat and walk'? But I want you to know that the Son of Man has authority on earth to forgive sins." So he said to the man, "I tell you, get up, take your mat and go home." He got up, took his mat and walked out in full view of them all. This amazed everyone and they praised God, saying, "We have never seen anything like this!" Mark 2:3-12

To the crowd, all this man needed was physical healing. However, Jesus knew that there were deeper issues that needed addressing first: forgiveness. Once that need had been attended to, the physical healing followed. Like this story, God wants to heal us completely, inside and out.

Forgiveness from God follows our repentance. For God to bring newness of life into an area of our lives, we first need to be willing to get rid of the old. If you pour new wine into old wineskins, they will burst. The old and the new cannot reside together. By way of example, if someone is suffering from an addiction, then the individual will first need to get to the place where they sincerely want to be free from it, and, importantly, that they repent. In ministry I have met people who have a desire to be free from an addiction but are just not ready to give it up. In such cases, the best thing to pray is that God will help that person get to the place where they are willing to turn their back on it. Unless they are willing to change, they cannot be set free. The heart must be willing.

For those who are so desperate they are willing to repent, then God will be able to completely deliver that person from the addiction. Not only can God set the person free from the addiction, but He can also heal the physical problems they may have encountered from the years of abusing their bodies including healing of physical scars, unhealthy eating habits, and sicknesses (including hepatitis and sexually transmitted diseases). If the addiction has been gambling, then God can provide them the professional help they need to lift themselves out of debt. God has a wonderful way of restoring the broken areas of our lives. Healing mental trauma will likely take more time as God will need to take someone through a process of renewing of the mind.

Whatever the sin, God can completely transform someone's life from it if they are ready and willing, and forgiveness and physical healing will follow.

Forgiving others

Some people have not yet received their physical healing because they have not yet obeyed Christ's command to forgive. Healing evangelist, Carlos Annacondia, has seen countless times when someone chose to forgive someone who hurt them and how their own physical healing followed. Here is one testimony he shares in his book:

> In 1994 I was invited to the annual conference of the Danish Assemblies. I preached on the power of forgiveness. There was a young man on crutches who caught my attention. He came up to the altar and shouted while crying, "I forgive my father. Lord, I forgive my father." A few minutes later, I saw him throwing the

crutches on the floor and running up to the platform to give his testimony. God had healed him! [10]

Annacondia describes how God enabled this young man to realize he needed to forgive his father of the wrongs he had done to him as a child, and with God's help, he did. What followed that act of obedience was a dramatic release of God's healing power into his physical body. God healed him completely both inwardly and outwardly. God wants to heal not only our physical pains and ailments, but our inner pain and wounds too.

If you are struggling with forgiving someone, you may find chapter seven helpful where I explain about the subject in more depth.

Inner healing

Some physical problems we experience may be the result of an inner wound that hasn't been dealt with yet. If that is the case, the inner wound may need to be addressed and healed first before the physical healing can take place.

Anyone who has experienced some kind of trauma or suffering in their background, will often need inner healing. It's easy to discern if this is the case: are you perhaps over-sensitive in certain areas? Are there things that trigger an overstated negative reaction in you? Do you experience nightmares or anxiety or depression or a debilitating fear? These are often signs that inner healing is needed. This was the case for me. The first healing process God ever took me through after I came to first know God as a teenager was inner healing. It took a few years for me to realize I needed healing from rejection, but when I did, I sought after it and

---

[10] *Listen to me Satan: Keys for Breaking the Devil's Grip and Bringing Revival to Your World*, p.106

God kindly provided. He counselled me through His Word, and through seeking Him in prayer, God brought inner healing by His Holy Spirit. He can do the same for you.

So many have gone through painful experiences in their lives, and it makes sense that God would want to heal our inner wounds, as they can hold us back from enjoying the fullness of life and our life's purpose. Areas of healing include low self-worth, identity issues, insecurity, fears, rejection, various forms of abuse, painful memories, lack of confidence, unforgiveness, anger or rebellion, distrust, trauma and so on. If you think you may need inner healing, God can gently and lovingly take you through a healing process at a pace that you can handle. God will first help you understand that you need healing, and then take you through a gentle step by step process towards that.

You don't need to stay as you are. God can heal us of any inner wound or trauma. As someone who has seen the difference inner healing can make, I would encourage you to seek God for it. God can really transform how you feel and think and how you react to situations. God wants to heal your inner wounds and transform your life for the better. To begin, ask God to show you if there is an area that needs dealing with and ask Him to take you through a healing process. God the Holy Spirit will gently and lovingly guide you through that. God is your Wonderful Counsellor and wants to heal all the scars and wounds from the past. Allow Him to counsel you and heal your heart and mind.

If you think you may need inner healing, start by spending time with God in prayer and reading the Bible. Tell Him how you feel. That might not be easy at first, so ask God to help you do that. If you struggle to talk to God, write it down as a prayer. I remember a period in my twenties when for some reason, I just couldn't pray verbally. So I started writing down my prayers instead. This went on for around six months until I was able to pray out loud again.

However you pray, don't be afraid of telling God how you honestly feel. Nothing will surprise or shock Him. He's loving and big enough to handle whatever you say. Talking to God honestly in prayer about how you feel is a very important part of the healing process. As you open your heart to God, God will speak back to you.

God brings healing and transformation by the power of His Holy Spirit and through the counsel of His Word

The Bible describes the Holy Spirit as our Counsellor, Comforter and Helper, who knows just the right words of healing and counsel we need. As you share with God your thoughts, He will share with you His words of healing, comfort and truth you need to hear:

> "And I [Jesus] will pray the Father, and he shall give you another Comforter, that he may abide with you for ever; Even the Spirit of truth" John 14:16-17 (KJV). See also John 14:26; 15:26; and 16:7.

> "For unto us a child is born, unto us a son is given: and the government shall be upon his shoulder: and his name shall be called Wonderful, Counsellor, The mighty God, The everlasting Father, The Prince of Peace." Isaiah 9:6 (KJV)

Although a human counsellor can be a great help, enabling someone to recognize and understand an issue, God is the very best Counsellor and the only One who can heal us completely. God knows exactly what we need to hear and how to minister His healing into our hurting hearts and minds.

PART C

God will guide you step by step, counselling you all the way through to healing. Reading God's Word and prayer are a very important part of that, and He will minister to your heart and mind and heal your wounds by His Holy Spirit. He is very gentle but also very powerful. He is the very best Counsellor and Healer.

One area of inner healing that might be needed is correcting what you believe about yourself, others and even God. The enemy is the father of lies as we have looked at previously and does a good job of convincing people of lies about themselves and God, making them feel undervalued and unloved. Going through life holding to such mistaken beliefs will keep us down and hold us back. We really need to learn what the Bible has to say about how God feels about us and how valuable we are to Him.

On the following page are some Bible truths about how God feels about you. Please read it through and ask God to speak to your heart and mind. If something particularly stands out, pray about that. Believe what God's Word says about you and not what the enemy of our souls may have convinced you of.

Truth statement	Promise of the Bible
I am of great value to God	Are not five sparrows sold for two pennies? Yet not one of them is forgotten by God. Indeed, the very hairs of your head are all numbered. Don't be afraid; you are worth more than many sparrows. Luke 12:6–7
I am loved by God	See what great love the Father has lavished on us, that we should be called children of God! 1 John 3:1
God has a purpose for my life	For we are God's handiwork, created in Christ Jesus to do good works, which God prepared in advance for us to do. Ephesians 2:10
I can receive clear guidance from God	Trust in the LORD with all your heart and lean not on your own understanding; in all your ways submit to him, and he will make your paths straight." Prov 3:5–6.
I have strength in God	I can do everything through Christ, who gives me strength. Philippians 4:13
God will meet my needs	But seek first his kingdom and his righteousness, and all these things will be given to you as well. Matthew 6:33
God cares about me	Cast all your anxiety on him because he cares for you. 1 Peter 5:7
I am washed clean from my past	He saved us through the washing of rebirth and renewal by the Holy Spirit. Titus 3:5

PART C

God wants you transform your mind, heart, body, and soul. The woman in the following Bible story experienced this. She had a history but came to understand God's love and grace for her, and her whole life was transformed as a result. God gave her a brand-new start:

> "When one of the Pharisees [religious leaders] invited Jesus to have dinner with him, he went to the Pharisee's house and reclined at the table. A woman in that town who lived a sinful life learned that Jesus was eating at the Pharisee's house, so she came there with an alabaster jar of perfume. As she stood behind him at his feet weeping, she began to wet his feet with her tears. Then she wiped them with her hair, kissed them and poured perfume on them.
> When the Pharisee who had invited him saw this, he said to himself, 'If this man were a prophet, he would know who is touching him and what kind of woman she is—that she is a sinner.'
> Jesus answered him, 'Simon, I have something to tell you.'
> 'Tell me, teacher,' he said.
> 'Two people owed money to a certain moneylender. One owed him five hundred denarii, and the other fifty. Neither of them had the money to pay him back, so he forgave the debts of both. Now which of them will love him more?'
> Simon replied, I suppose the one who had the bigger debt forgiven.'
> 'You have judged correctly,' Jesus said.
> Then he turned toward the woman and said to Simon, 'Do you see this woman? I came into your house. You did not give me any water for my feet, but she wet my feet with her tears and wiped them with her hair. You did not give me a kiss, but this woman, from the time I entered, has not stopped kissing my feet. You did not

put oil on my head, but she has poured perfume on my feet. Therefore, I tell you, her many sins have been forgiven—as her great love has shown. But whoever has been forgiven little loves little.'
Then Jesus said to her, 'Your sins are forgiven…. Your faith has saved you; go in peace'". Luke 7:36-48 and 50

Not all women become promiscuous for mere pleasure. It's often out of a longing for love and acceptance. They may have experienced some form of abuse as a child or young adult, damaging their self-worth and identity, and end up in a lifestyle they wish they could break free from. This happens to men too. For others, they may have been trafficked and enslaved against their will by a captor. Although the woman in the story had a reputation of being a sinner to those who knew her, in Christ's eyes, she was dearly loved and forgiven. The teachings of Christ and the merciful compassion of God the Father healed her broken heart and life. She received revelation of how much God loved and forgave her, which is why she was so grateful to her Saviour. More grateful than those watching.

Don't judge someone by what you see. You never know what experiences they've been through that led to where they are now. Like this woman, perhaps you've been judged by others, perhaps even by religious people. Maybe you've been misunderstood and rejected. You may have even suffered enslavement. Whatever you story, God wants you to know *how much He loves and accepts you*. You are so loved by God! No matter what you've been through in life till now, God can give heal those wounds and give you a brand-new start. He can give you a wonderful future plan. God will never shun or reject you like others may have done. God loves you with an everlasting love and He has a wonderful purpose for your life. You are welcomed by God. Don't listen to the negative voices around you. Listen to God's truth as the Bible reveals and start walking into your new life.

As Jesus Himself said in Mark 2:17, He is the doctor of our souls, bringing healing, forgiveness, and freedom into those sick areas of our lives. As He pointed out, it's not the healthy who need a doctor but the sick, whom He came to heal. As you pray and ask God to heal you and speak to you through His Word and Holy Spirit, you too will receive God's wonderful healing touch and discover God's love and purpose for your life, bringing complete healing and hope.

No matter what you've been through in life, don't allow your past to dictate your future. Ask God to take you through a process of inner healing. You will be utterly amazed at how God will transform your life for the better. He is able to do far more than you can ask or even imagine (Ephesians 3:20).

To develop your faith in God

Another reason why we may not yet have received healing is because our faith needs to be strengthened. After all, it is through faith that God's power is released.

In chapter two, I shared how God recently healed me from a painful lump in my breast. At the start of that journey, I knew I didn't have enough faith for healing, so I decided to immerse my heart in His Word to grow my faith. For a week, God ministered to my heart and strengthened my faith through Matthew 9:28–30a:

> When he had gone indoors, the blind men came to him, and he asked them, "Do you believe that I am able to do this?" "Yes, Lord." they replied. Then he touched their eyes and said, "According to your faith will it be done to you"; and their sight was restored.

I wanted God to heal me and so allowed God to strengthen and encourage my faith through His Word, which He did. Probably many of us reading these words may not feel our faith is where it needs to be for healing. Don't be discouraged. Faith is like a muscle. The more we strengthen it, the stronger it grows. As we immerse our hearts and minds in the promises of God's Word, our faith grows and is strengthened as Romans 10:17 (ESV) talks about:

> "So faith comes from hearing, and hearing through the word of Christ."

Faith comes from hearing God's Word. God's truth imparts faith to our hearts and minds. That's why it's so important to read God's Word to understand what His will is and to strengthen our faith needed for healing:

> And a great crowd followed him and thronged about him. And there was a woman who had had a discharge of blood for twelve years, and who had suffered much under many physicians, and had spent all she had, and was no better but rather grew worse. She had heard the reports about Jesus and came up behind him in the crowd and touched his garment. For she said, "If I touch even his garments, I will be made well." And immediately the flow of blood dried up, and she felt in her body that she was healed of her disease. And Jesus, perceiving in himself that power had gone out from him, immediately turned about in the crowd and said, "Who touched my garments?" And his disciples said to him, "You see the crowd pressing around you, and yet you say, 'Who touched me?'" And he looked around to see who had done it. But the woman, knowing what had happened to her, came in fear and trembling and fell down before him and told him the whole truth. And

he said to her, "Daughter, your faith has made you well; go in peace, and be healed of your disease." Mark 5: 24 to 34 (ESV)

"Are any of you suffering hardships? You should pray. Are any of you happy? You should sing praises. Are any of you sick? You should call for the elders of the church to come and pray over you, anointing you with oil in the name of the Lord. Such a prayer offered in faith will heal the sick, and the Lord will make you well." James 5:13-15

In all of these Scriptures, faith was the conduit for God's healing to flow. Previously in chapter six we looked at the importance of faith to see answers to prayer and what faith in God actually looks like. Faith pleases God (Hebrews 11:6). It may well be that we haven't yet received our answer to prayer because we don't have the full assurance of faith needed:

"Now faith is the substance of things hoped for, the evidence of things not seen." Hebrews 11:1 (NKJV)

There needs to be substance and evidence of our faith. Only then is it the kind of faith that moves mountains. Faith is not passive but takes risks. The woman in Mark 5 took a risk to touch Jesus' garments. She shouldn't have been in the crowd at all as she would have been classed as unclean in her culture. But she didn't care. She was desperate to do whatever it took to obtain her healing from Jesus.

We need to put all our hope in God. To encourage your faith for healing, I have provided one-month of devotional Bible readings on healing and prayer at the back of this book. I suggest reading a scripture a day, mediating on God's powerful promises, allowing God to speak and minister to your heart. As you work through the scriptures, you will find your faith and confidence in God building, which will create the fertile ground for healing. We all need our faith encouraged. Put all your hope in God's promises.

To learn how to rely on God

Renowned Christian theologian and author, C.S. Lewis, once wrote,

> *God allows us to experience the low points of life in order to teach us lessons that we could learn no other way.*

Paul the apostle found this to be true and elaborated this point in 2 Corinthians 1:8-10 (ESV):

> "For we do not want you to be unaware, brothers, of the affliction we experienced in Asia. For we were so utterly burdened beyond our strength that we despaired of life itself. Indeed, we felt that we had received the sentence of death. But that was to make us rely not on ourselves but on God who raises the dead. He delivered us from such a deadly peril, and he will deliver us. On him we have sent our hope that he will deliver us again."

God wants you to learn how faithful He is and how powerful and able He is to help and deliver you through your trials, no matter how mountainous your trials may be. When we are going through the storms of life, these are golden opportunities to experience God and learn how good and faithful He is. If we will seek God in the midst of our suffering, we discover He is there with us, ready to strengthen, encourage and deliver us.

Learning to trust and rely on God for help and deliverance is one of the greatest lessons we all need to learn. Once you've experienced God's help and intervention, your faith will never be the same. You will have more confidence the next time a trial comes round. Learning to trust in God will protect your heart and mind from worry and anxiety.

God allowed Paul and his companions to experience great trouble, to the point that they thought they were going to die. Yet God used the painful trial they were going through to teach them how they could truly trust and rely on God to rescue them, which He did. They learned firsthand how faithful God is and grew in confidence that God would deliver them again in the future.

If we rely on ourselves or others to get us through the problems we face, how we will ever learn how powerful and faithful God is? God calls us to trust Him with all our hearts and not rely on our own, limited understanding of things (Proverbs 3:5,6). Experiencing God moving in your life in answer to prayer is one of the greatest joys in life, firming up our faith and confidence in God when future troubles rear their head. Allow God to teach you to rely on Him and you will see Him help and rescue you.

Prayers for healing

Now that we've looked at how it is God's will to heal us and addressed blockages that can hinder that, let's move on to look at how to actually pray for healing.

Pray wisely

At this point, I want to mention that we need to give some attention to what we actually pray for. I mentioned earlier in the book how God healed me of heart palpitations I was experiencing at night. However, I didn't think to pray for the palpitations I occasionally had in the day because by comparison, they were far fewer and not so bad and so they continued. From that, I learned that you get what you pray for!

My husband also had a similar experience when he prayed for his daughter when she became unwell:

> Isabel was around seven years old and was complaining that her stomach was hurting. I took her to the doctor who then said I should rush her to hospital as he diagnosed appendicitis. I drove her to the hospital as fast as I could with one hand on the steering wheel and one hand on my daughter, commanding the pain to leave and for God's protection over her in the name of Jesus Christ.
>
> We were at hospital for 24 hours and I just sat with her, praying constantly for the pain would stop and that she would be safe and not die. We had four doctors see her at the hospital who were totally confused as to what was wrong with her because by now the pain was pretty much gone.
>
> The doctors couldn't decide what to do. Some thought it was appendicitis and others didn't because of the lack of pain. They were arguing with each other as to what was wrong with her until they finally decided two days later to do an exploratory. They discovered that not only had her appendix burst, but it had by now shrivelled away as it had been some time since it had burst. This again baffled them as they said she should have died from the infection caused by this. She suffered no consequences, no damage to her organs, no harm whatsoever, which the doctors said would be impossible. God answered my prayers just as I asked.

God answered Anthony's prayers just as he prayed. However, the lack of pain baffled the doctors and as a result it took them a few days to decide to do the exploratory. In the meantime, her appendix had burst which can have life-threatening complications. Thankfully Anthony had also prayed for God's protection and that she would not die. My point is, pay some attention to what you pray for and pray wisely. For example, if you're going to pray for a leg to grow in length, pray it grows to the same length as the other.

If you're going to pray healing with someone else, always do a little investigation first. Perhaps they have a problem in one part of their body, but the pain is radiating elsewhere. Don't just pray for the pain to leave. Pray that God would heal the problem that's causing the pain in the first place. I have also found that someone will ask for prayer about one problem but not mention another more serious problem. Or that someone needs healing for an issue but fail to mention what caused it in the first place, such as an accident or trauma of some kind.

It's important to try to understand what is causing the problem so you know how to pray most effectively. If someone did have a negative experience of some kind, spiritual healing may also be needed as well as physical. So don't just rush in. Ask a few questions to understand the fuller picture. By way of example, it's like someone going to their doctor for ongoing headaches. The doctor provides medication which seem to have some effect, but the real problem is a dental issue. Their symptoms will not be cured until the problem in the mouth is sorted. Be wise how you pray.

Pray in the name of Jesus Christ

The most important thing to remember when praying for healing is to pray in the authority of the name of Jesus Christ. We pray in Christ's name is because as we have seen, He is the One who has made healing possible through His sacrifice on the cross, paying for our sins and sicknesses, and defeating the powers of the Devil by His resurrection. It is Christ's power and authority at work, and we can ask Him for anything in His name as He taught in John 16:24:

"Until now you have not asked for anything in my name. Ask and you will receive, and your joy will be complete."

If you wish to pray for healing for yourself or someone else, speak directly to the ailment and declare specifically what you want to happen in the name of Jesus Christ. You can pray for yourself or pray for others as all believers are invited to ask for anything in Christ's name. Below are some suggested prayers below that you may wish to use.

Suggested prayers

In Christ's name you have authority to command sickness and pain to leave. There is no need or reason to be shy or reserved, so don't hold back.

Thank you Father God, for your healing power and love. In the authority of the name of Jesus Christ, *[name the sickness / pain]*, I command you to leave right now and never return. *[Pain / sickness]* I rebuke you in the name of Jesus Christ. Almighty God deliver me from the evil one and may your kingdom come, and your will be done in my life. Amen.

Be specific and name the sickness you are commanding to leave, speaking directly to it. Personally, I like to use the word 'command' because it drives home that we are exercising Christ's authority. If you have the gift of tongues, always follow the Holy Spirit's lead and use the prayer gift.

Creative miracles

I remember in one Bible study at my church some years ago, there was an unbeliever there who said she would like us to pray for her back. She was having problems because one leg was about an inch shorter than the other, causing back problems as a result. We decided that we would get to the crux of the problem and ask God to lengthen the shorter leg, so they were equal in length, which would solve her back problems. So that's what we did. In the name of Jesus Christ, we commanded the shorter leg to grow to the same length as the other, and God answered. There were two other non-believers sat on the sofa watching this and when they saw the leg grow, one of them leapt off the sofa, shocked and shouted, "Her leg grew, her leg grew!". I love it when God answers prayer and I couldn't help but smile. God grew her leg and faith in God also grew in the room as a result.

If it's a creative miracle that is therefore needed, you can pray like this:

Thank you almighty God, for your healing power and love. In the authority of the name of Jesus Christ, I command the *right leg to grow to the same length as the left leg / middle ear to be formed / new disc to appear / new back muscle to be formed / new bone to grow / new kneecap to form / metal to disappear in place of new bone etc.* **Thank you, LORD, amen.**

For some physical problems and sicknesses (not all), there can be an unclean spirit at work as Jesus revealed through some of His miracles. In such cases, you need to make sure the open door to the enemy has been firmly shut and that any unforgiveness, sin, generational curse etc., has been dealt with. We will address this in the next two chapters.

Questions for further study

1. Look at the 31-day devotional plan for healing in the appendix. Is there a verse that stands out to you?

2. Do you know anyone who experienced a miraculous healing? What happened?

3. Why do you think healings and miracles are important for today?

4. Why do you think God sometimes needs to do an inner work of healing before physical healing is obtained?

5. Please read Psalm 103:1-18. What are some of the blessings from knowing God? Have you experienced any of these?

6. Now read Philippians 4:6-7. What does the Bible teach we should do when we suffer from anxiety? What is the outcome of that?

7. Do you need prayer for healing? Take some time to pray for that now.

Chapter 10

Freedom from curses

"I will bless those who bless you, and whoever curses you I will curse." Genesis 12:3

Another important area we need to consider that could cause problems physically, spiritually or even practically, is being under a curse. These are invisible barriers that can block the blessing of God. If you have been praying for God's healing or blessing, but nothing seems to be happening, it would be worth considering whether a curse is at work.

Curses are an invisible barrier that block the healing power and blessings of God from flowing into your life.

When one thinks about being blessed, one thinks of prosperity, increase and a healthy life and well-being. To be cursed however, is the very opposite. The word *bless* and its associated use occurs over 500 times in the Bible, and the word *curse* over 200. That's a lot of mentions about a subject many of us know little about.

How curses can be brought on

Curses are very real and can be brought on in a number of different ways. They could be brought on through no fault of our own, or as a result of our own words or conduct.

Cursed by someone

A curse can be brought on from being cursed by someone who is aggrieved as the following Bible passages talk about:

> "With the tongue we praise our Lord and Father, and with it we curse human beings, who have been made in God's likeness. Out of the same mouth come praise and cursing. My brothers and sisters, this should not be. Can both fresh water and salt water flow from the same spring?" James 3:9-11

> "So David and his men continued along the road while Shimei was going along the hillside opposite him, cursing as he went and throwing stones at him and showering him with dirt." 2 Samuel 16:13

> "When Noah awoke from his wine and found out what his youngest son had done to him, he said, 'Cursed be Canaan! The lowest of slaves will he be to his brothers.'" Genesis 9:24,25

> "His [Job] wife said to him, 'Are you still maintaining your integrity? Curse God and die!" Job 2:10

In each of these instances, an offended person is cursing another through their spoken words. This is not how God wants us to treat each other. The Bible teaches that if our enemies have mistreated us, we are to bless and not curse them. It is God's job to avenge us and deal with our enemies.

Instead, we are commanded to overcome evil with good (Romans 12:21).

I remember witnessing a woman speak a curse over a man who was not aware at the time of what she was doing. I knew that this woman had a history in witchcraft. Although I didn't understand at the time of what was going on, it became clear later on when the curse began to manifest. The woman had cursed the man with death.

Some months later, that man developed unbearable pain in his body, which following medical tests, hospital staff could find no reason for. In a dream, God revealed that it was the result of a curse, and so he took authority over that curse and broke it in the name of Jesus Christ. He was immediately healed and has never experienced those symptoms since.

Just be aware that there are people who seek revenge by invoking curses, even spells, over others. God clearly forbids such practices:

> "Let no one be found among you who sacrifices their son or daughter in the fire, or who practices divination or sorcery, interprets omens, engages in witchcraft, or casts spells, or who is a medium or spiritist or who consults the dead. Anyone who does these things is detestable to the LORD." Deuteronomy 18:10-12a

If you think you may be the victim of a curse, just remember that the name of Jesus Christ is the most powerful name in heaven and earth and has the authority to break every curse. You have no reason to be afraid for God is far greater and will lead you into victory in every circumstance. Walk in power and confidence in Christ.

Cursing yourself

It is also possible to bring on a curse over yourself through the words you speak over your life. For example, by saying to yourself things like, 'I'll never have children' or 'I'll never be well'. Someone I know who had been invited to jury service but didn't want to attend, told people she was going to give the excuse that her ankle was broken so she wouldn't have to appear. Lo and behold, a week later she had an accident and to her surprise, she actually did break her ankle. She had basically cursed herself. The Bible makes it clear how powerful words can be:

> "Death and life are in the power of the tongue and those who love it will eat its fruit." Proverbs 18:21

> "There is one who speaks like the piercings of a sword, but the tongue of the wise promotes health." Proverbs 12:18

The Bible emphasises the tremendous power of the tongue to do good or to bring harm. We need to be careful to not knowingly or unknowingly speak a curse over ourselves or others. We need to be careful with our words.

Steve

Steve's family reached out to me when he was at death's door in hospital. His organs were shutting down and it was thought he only probably had a day, perhaps a few at most to live. The medical staff just didn't know what was causing his physical problems. When I heard that, I suspected it was spiritual. That is often the case when doctors don't know the cause of someone's physical problems.

I didn't know Steve personally and so I had nothing to go on in terms of knowing how to pray for him most effectively.

However, I learned that he was a fan of a particular death metal band. I looked up the lyrics to some of their songs, and sure enough, they were dark. I realised that he had probably brought a curse on himself by singing these words, probably bringing on a spirit of death. I immediately went to prayer and in the powerful name of Jesus Christ, I rebuked the spirit of death over him, commanding that evil spirit to leave him and never return. In prayer, I also broke every plan and scheme of the enemy to destroy him and I broke any curse that might be at work in his life. Then I commanded healing into his body in Christ's name. I prayed that God would deliver him from the evil one, and for God's kingdom to come and God's will to be done in his life as Jesus taught us to pray. And I prayed fervently using the gift of tongues.

The next day his family told me he had done a dramatic U-turn. From that day on, he made a steady recovery.

If you are suffering from a physical problem that perhaps modern medicine isn't really touching or can't diagnose, I would encourage you to seek God to see if there is a curse at work. Ask God to show you the cause, and deal with that in prayer.

Cursed as a result of sin and disobedience

A third way we can find ourselves under a curse is because of our own sin and disobedience. The following Bible passages warn about the danger of this:

> "Cursed is anyone who makes an idol – a thing detestable to the LORD, the work of skilled hands – and sets it up in secret." Deuteronomy 27:15

> "Cursed is anyone who dishonours his father or mother." Deuteronomy 27:16

> "If you do not listen, and if you do not resolve to honour my name," says the LORD Almighty, "I will send a curse on you, and I will curse your blessings. Yes, I have already cursed them, because you have not resolved to honour me." Malachi 2:2

> "Cursed is anyone who withholds justice from the foreigner, the fatherless or the widow." Deuteronomy 27:19

> "Cursed is the one who trusts in man, who draws strength from mere flesh and whose heart turns away from the LORD." Jeremiah 17:5

> "Will a mere mortal rob God? Yet you rob me. But you ask, 'How are we robbing you?' 'In tithes and offerings. You are under a curse – your whole nation – because you are robbing me.'" Malachi 3:8-9

All of these passages show that we can bring ourselves under a curse from sinning towards God or our fellow man. God cares about how we treat others, and is also passionate about our devotion to Him. One portion of Scripture where this is particularly emphasised is Deuteronomy 27 and 28. In these chapters, God talks at length about the potential blessings and curses His people the Israelites could receive. Whether they experienced blessings or curses would entirely depend on their own choices and how they chose to live. There isn't room to list everything here, but here is an excerpt from God's dialogue:

> "If you fully obey the LORD your God and carefully follow all his commands I give you today, the LORD your God will set you high above all the nations on earth. All these blessings will come on you and accompany you if you obey the LORD your God:

You will be blessed in the city and blessed in the country. The fruit of your womb will be blessed, and the crops of your land and the young of your livestock – the calves of your herds and the lambs of your flocks. Your basket and your kneading trough will be blessed. You will be blessed when you come in and blessed when you go out. The LORD will grant that the enemies who rise up against you will be defeated before you…
The LORD will send a blessing on your barns and on everything you put your hand to…
However, if you do not obey the LORD your God and do not carefully follows all his commands and decrees I am giving you today, all these curses will come on you and overtake you:
You will be cursed in the city and cursed in the country. Your basket and your kneading trough will be cursed. The fruit of your womb will be cursed, and the crops of your land, and the calves of your herds and the lambs of your flocks. You will be cursed when you come in and when you go out…" Deuteronomy 28:1-8 and 15-19

You get the idea. God talks at length about the many blessings He promised to bring on His people following their obedience, but also the potential curses they could come under if they turned away from Him and walked in sinful disobedience. The blessings and curses would impact their work, fertility, health (including mental health) and relationships. I encourage you to read those chapters.

These passages are not only relevant to the people of Israel for through our disobedience, but we too can also bring ourselves under a curse. It is God's desire to bless His people in all areas of their lives. However, the Bible is clear that blessings are conditional and explains that if people engage in sins such as worshipping other gods, ignoring the plight of the poor and needy, engaging in occult practices, sexual immorality, murder or injustice, even dishonouring one's parents, God will remove His blessings and people can bring themselves under a curse. The impact of blessings and curses can also extend beyond the individual, to families, communities, nations, and can even be passed down through generations. These are sobering truths.

Now that we are the New Covenant through the sacrifice and shed blood of Jesus Christ, as we repent, we are forgiven and set free from the consequences of any curse, which Jesus made possible by becoming a curse for us in our place:

> "Christ redeemed us from the curse of the law by becoming a curse for us – for it is written, 'Cursed is everyone who is hanged on a tree'". Galatians 3:13

Because of what Christ has done for us, we can be set free from any curse. If someone is continually experiencing ongoing negative circumstances, a lack of blessing in their practical lives, or ongoing problems in other areas without positive change even after prayer, consider whether a curse might be operational and address it in prayer.

The importance of repentance

If someone is refusing to deal with sin, then the curse will remain. I know fellow believers who have refused to acknowledge and repent of a particular ongoing sin and as a result, they are not experiencing the freedom and healing God wants for them.

Unless you repent, the Devil retains that foothold in your life from which he can afflict you as we saw in the previously. That's why repentance is essential as then you are giving that area back to God for His control and protection. Some people are not experiencing freedom simply because they mistakenly believe God has forgiven them for sins they have not repented of. They don't realise that repentance, as well as faith, is a requirement to experiencing God's forgiveness through Christ:

> "Repent and be baptised every one of you in the name of Jesus Christ for the forgiveness of your sins, and you will receive the gift of the Holy Spirit." Acts 2:38

> "Repent therefore, and turn back, that your sins may be blotted out, that times of refreshing may come from the presence of the Lord…" Acts 3:19

Sin is one of the biggest reasons why some people bring themselves under a curse and remain there. I'm not talking about the occasional slip up, but ongoing, defining behaviour. If you're still persistently walk in sin, you won't be able to find freedom in an area until you repent.

Cursed objects

Yet another way we can find ourselves under an unfortunate curse is by bringing a cursed object into your home. Examples include ornaments that have been involved in idol worship, or objects that represent an idol such as a wall hanging with a dragon, or a statue of an object that is worshipped. If you have a statue of buddha in your home or garden, get rid of it. You may not be worshipping it, but it represents a false deity and you may bring a curse upon yourself with it being in your home:

> "The carved images of their gods you shall burn with fire. You shall not covet the silver or the gold that is on them or take it for yourselves, lest you be ensnared by it, for it is an abomination to the LORD your God. And you shall not bring an abominable thing into your house and become devoted to destruction like it. You shall utterly

detest and abhor it, for it is devoted to destruction." Deuteronomy 7:25-26 (ESV)

Why take the chance?

Generational curses

Another way your life may be affected by a curse is from a curse being passed down from an ancestor. Many of us have no idea what our ancestors did or what they were involved in. If there is a hereditary physical problem in your family that is being passed down, it might be worth considering whether a curse may be at work. For example, numerous people in a family with the same hearing issues or heart defect. Ask God to break any generational curse and set you and your family free.

If you know an ancestor has been involved in some kind of magic or the occult, false religion, or even freemasonry, then there will likely be a generational curse at work that will need to be confessed to God and repented of. Ask for God's forgiveness for your ancestor and command the curse be broken in the name of Jesus Christ. Even though you may not have engaged in that yourself, its consequences may have been passed down your family and will need to be addressed and cut off.

Prayer for freedom from curses

Whatever the cause of the curse, don't hesitate to break it in the name of Jesus Christ, asking God to set you free. You may wish to use the prayer below. If you feel you need help with this, ask a mature Christian from your church to pray with you. Unless a curse is broken, it will remain and continue to cause problems. Jesus Christ hung on the cross and became a curse for us that we might be forgiven, set free from every curse, and blessed. Jesus died our death that we might share in His life. God wants you to be blessed, not cursed. He wants to set you free. Nothing is too difficult for God.

Dear Heavenly Father God, thank you for your love and healing power in my life. I repent of my sins and ask for your forgiveness. In the all-powerful authority and name of Jesus Christ, I now break every curse over my life: every generational curse, every self-inflicted curse and every curse caused by others. Almighty God, set me free from the power and consequences of every curse I pray. I declare that no weapon that's formed against me will prosper. Fill my life with your Holy Spirit and pour your healing into my body, soul, mind, and spirit. Deliver me from the evil one and may your kingdom come, and your will be done in my life. Thank you so much for setting me free. In the name of Jesus Christ, I pray, amen.

Questions for further study

1. Has God highlighted something in this chapter to you that you think He is calling you to deal with?

2. Is there an area of your life you have been praying about for some time and have not yet experienced freedom in? If yes, what is that?

3. After reading this chapter, do you think you might know how to address that?

4. Do you know if any of your ancestors were involved in the occult, spiritualism or Freemasonry? If yes, please take the time to address that in prayer.

5. Do you think you might be under a curse? If so, take some time to deal with that in prayer.

6. Is there an ongoing sin in your life that you have not yet repented of? Are you ready to deal with that now?

7. Take some time and ask God to pour out His blessings on your life.

Chapter 11

How to pray for deliverance: Five Steps to freedom

"For though we walk in the flesh, we are not waging war according to the flesh. For the weapons of our warfare are not of the flesh but have divine power to destroy strongholds." 2 Corinthians 10:3,4

If you think you may be suffering from some kind of oppression or affliction caused by an unclean spirit, then this chapter will show you how you can be set free. This is a very important step towards becoming healed and whole in your life.

The first and most important fact we need to remember is that God has given those who trust in Jesus Christ as their Lord and Saviour authority and power over all the power of the evil one. Let's make it clear: Satan and his evil minions are defeated. Christ overcame the power of sin and death through His own death and resurrection, and Satan was disarmed as a result as Colossians 2:14-15 (NLT) explain:

"Then God made you alive with Christ, for he forgave all our sins. He cancelled the record of the charges against us and took it away by nailing it to the cross. In this way, he [Jesus Christ] *disarmed the spiritual rulers and authorities. He shamed them publicly by his victory over them on the cross."* (author's emphasis)

If any enemy is disarmed, it means that they've been defeated, and their weapons deactivated and neutralised. In the same way, Jesus Christ defeated and disarmed Satan and his evil forces through His victory at the cross and resurrection, which means you can implement the power and victory of Christ when you pray in His name. You are on the winning side and have nothing to fear. As a child of God, you can experience victory in your life, which Christ has accomplished for us:

"But thanks be to God, who gives us victory through our Lord Jesus Christ." 1 Corinthians 15:57

As we have looked at before, when Christ returned to God the Father after His resurrection, He commanded His followers to continue the same work He did whilst He walked this earth, healing the sick and setting free the oppressed:

"And these signs will accompany those who believe: In my name they will drive out demons; they will speak in new tongues; they will pick up snakes with their hands; and when they drink deadly poison, it will not hurt them at all; they will place their hands on sick people, and they will get well." Mark 16:17-18

As a follower of Jesus Christ, that includes you. You have the power and authority in Christ to rebuke unclean spirits. So much of Christ's work involved this work as evil spirits often caused physical problems too, and this work of the evil one hasn't gone away.

Going through the following process will bring the freedom you need. It's straightforward to deal with in the name of Jesus Christ, and you'll be amazed at the positive difference it will make to your life.

There are five important steps in this process to freedom:

1. Place your faith in Jesus Christ
2. Confess any sin to God and repent
3. Forgive those who've wronged you
4. Break any connection with occult practices and false religions
5. Command the unclean spirits to leave

If you are ready to proceed, let's begin and go through each step towards freedom.

Step 1: Place your faith in Jesus Christ

> "Jesus answered, 'I am the way and the truth and the life. No one comes to the Father except through me.'" John 14:6

Jesus Christ declared there is no other way to God except through faith in Him. There are no other gods or religions that do what Jesus does: forgive all your sins, give you a friendship with God, save you from the power of sin, death, and hell, and bless you with eternal life with God. Because He died for our sins, Jesus made it possible to be forgiven and reconciled with God our Father. We need to declare our faith in Jesus Christ with our mouths:

> "'The word is near you; it is in your mouth and in your heart,' that is, the message concerning faith that we proclaim: If you declare with your mouth, 'Jesus is Lord,' and believe in your heart that God raised him from the dead, you will be saved. For it is with your heart that you believe and are justified, and it is with your mouth that you profess your faith and are saved. As the Scripture says, 'Anyone who believes in him will never be put

to shame.' For there is no difference between Jew and Gentile – the same Lord is Lord of all and richly blesses all who call on him, for, 'Everyone who calls on the name of the Lord will be saved.'" Romans 10:8-13

If someone does not yet trust Jesus Christ as their Lord and Saviour, any freedom may only be temporary as Jesus warned in Matthew 12:43-45:

"When an impure spirit comes out of a person, it goes through arid places seeking rest and does not find it. Then it says, 'I will return to the house I left.' When it arrives, it finds the house unoccupied, swept clean and put in order. Then it goes and takes with it seven other spirits more wicked than itself, and they go in and live there. And the final condition of that person is worse than the first."

Because the 'house' was unoccupied, impure spirits took up occupancy again, making things worse than before. Once someone has been set free from spiritual oppression, they need to be filled with the Holy Spirit if they want to remain free. If their life remains spiritually empty, they are vulnerable to re-occupancy. Someone may end up in a worse state that they started out at.

If you haven't yet made that decision to follow Christ, you can do that now. The Bible says today is the day of salvation. You never know what will happen in your life from one day to the next. Put your life right before God and experience His love, forgiveness, and healing power. God says to you today:

"In the time of my favour I heard you, and in the day of salvation I helped you. I tell you, now is the time of God's favour, now is the day of salvation." 2 Corinthians 6:2

Here is a suggested prayer for salvation if you wish to take that step:

Prayer for forgiveness and salvation

Father God, thank you so much for sending your Son, Jesus Christ, to die in my place and pay the punishment for my sins. I now surrender my life to you and want to be part of your family. Thank you for Your great love for me. I repent of all my sins. Please forgive me and wipe away all my guilt and shame. Fill me with your Holy Spirit and fulfil Your good purposes in my life. Deliver me from evil and may Your kingdom come and Your will be done in my life. In the name of Jesus Christ I pray, amen.

Step 2: Confess any sin to God and repent

If you are already a believer but there is an area of ongoing sin in your life that still needs dealing with, now is the time to repent of that and put it right before God. Continuing in sin will hinder your healing.

Deliverance is not a substitute for repentance

In other words, don't try to circumvent repentance by seeking deliverance. It doesn't work that way. Deliverance is no substitute for repentance for unless we repent, we give an evil spirit authority to remain and influence. Repentance is key.

As we have looked at, Jesus Christ came to undo Satan's evil works, as we read in 1 John 3:8:

> "The one who does what is sinful is of the Devil, because the Devil has been sinning from the beginning. The

reason the Son of God appeared was to destroy the Devil's work."

God wants to set you free and undo the Devil's destructive work in your life. Whatever the Devil has thrown at you or tempted you with in your life, God can heal completely, setting you free, still fulfilling His amazing plans for your life. God is that wonderful and powerful.

I suggest taking a few moments in prayer to ask God to bring to your mind, by His Holy Spirit, any sin that needs to be dealt with. If God brings something to mind, confess that to God, repent and ask for God's forgiveness in Christ.

Sorting out the root causes of your spiritual problems, is in essence, closing the doors to the enemy in your life and taking back the ground he's stolen, surrendering it to God. When you're no longer walking in sin, and are walking in obedience to God, those unclean spirits have no right to re-enter. Just remember, it's important that once you've found freedom in Christ, you continue walking with God.

Suggested prayer:

Thank you, Father God, for your love and healing power in my life. Thank you that Jesus Christ died on the cross for my sins, and that I may be forgiven and set free from the works of the evil one. In the authority and name of Jesus Christ, I now confess the sin that I have done against you _____ (*name the sin*). I confess this to you now and wholeheartedly repent of it. In the name of Jesus Christ, please forgive me for this sin and wash me clean. In the name and authority of Jesus Christ, please set me free from every sin and its consequences. Deliver me from the evil one and may your kingdom come, and your will be done in my life. Fill my life with your Holy Spirit

and heal me, body, soul, mind, and spirit. Thank you so much for setting me free. In Christ's name I pray, amen.

Step 3: Forgive those who've wronged you

As we looked at in chapter seven, forgiving others is one of the best things you can do for yourself. The Bible clearly teaches that if we don't forgive others, God will not forgive us:

> "For if you forgive other people when they sin against you, your heavenly Father will also forgive you. But if you do not forgive others their sins, your Father will not forgive your sins." Matthew 6:14-15

If we don't forgive, we struggle with bitterness, resentment and anger, and harbouring these attitudes opens a door to the enemy to afflict us. A big reason why people experience various kinds of spiritual oppression by the enemy is due to unforgiveness and its related negative attitudes. Read what deliverance minister, Carlos Annacondia, writes on this subject of forgiving others in order to find freedom:

> "There are many causes of sickness…Seventy percent of the people who suffer spiritual problems and end up in our tent of deliverance have hatred, anger, and roots of bitterness in their hearts. These are among the main causes of sickness and oppression in people's lives. The vast majority receive physical healing when they find inner healing through forgiveness.
> Examine your heart. There may be hatred toward a spouse, a cousin, one of your relatives, a neighbour, a brother or a sister. Hatred and resentment bring punishment. Many times they are the main reason for

diseases that seem to have no origin. No matter the reason why you hate, Jesus forgave and told us to do the same. If we don't do it, we remain in condemnation and disobedience to His Word. Forgiveness is not a *feeling*; it is a *decision*. If you want to forgive, the Lord will help you do it.

I have prayed for people ruined by diseases who have received healing the moment they finished praying and confessing forgiveness. It's awesome how God's power operates through forgiveness. Don't allow the Devil to use your feelings to bring sickness into your life." [11]

This is a powerful truth we need to take to heart. Forgiving others will set you free. It will benefit you greatly to forgive. Ask God to show you if there is someone you need to forgive:

Father God, please bring to my mind anyone I need to forgive. In the name of Jesus Christ, amen.

If God brings someone to mind, then here is a suggested prayer you can pray to take that step of obedience:

Heavenly Father, you know the wrongs that _____ [name] did against me. What they did hurt me deeply. Lord, I choose today to forgive _____ for this wrong. I forgive them. I entrust this wrong into your hands and I ask you to deal with it. Please forgive me and heal me Father God in the name of Jesus Christ. Give me your peace and fill me with your Holy Spirit. May your kingdom come and your will be done in my life I pray, amen.

---

[11] Carlos Annacondia, *Listen to me Satan!*, page 62.

Forgiving others will enable God to forgive you, plus it will release God's healing power into your life, setting you free from what is oppressing you. Forgiving others will be a great blessing in your life.

Step 4: Break any connection with occult practices or false religion

This essentially is the same concept as step two, confessing sins to God. But I've created a separate step to deal with this subject as we often don't realise that these practices are displeasing to God and how much negative influence they can have in our lives.

Begin by praying and asking God to bring back to mind any practice or involvement you might have had, however minor, that He wants you to repent of. Even if it was just reading your horoscope or playing an occult game for fun when you were younger, it needs to be repented of, the door closed to the Devil, and the ground taken back. For others, it will be more serious involvement that needs to be dealt with. Examples of spiritual counterfeits that will need to be repented of and dealt with include:

Various types of magic, reiki healing, crystals, casting spells and curses, tarot cards, freemasonry, telepathy, hypnosis, nature worship, palm reading, fortune telling, blood pacts, sexual spirits, other religions, witchcraft, spirit guides, clairvoyance, spiritism, Satanism, dowsing, shamanism, scientology, levitation, reincarnation, reiki, Ouija board, sceanes, wicca, out of body experiences etc. Involvement with spiritualist churches or philosophical practices will also need repenting of.

You may wish to pray this prayer to ask God to help you remember anything you might have dabbled with:

Heavenly Father, please bring to my mind by your Holy Spirit, anything I have done that involves the occult, or false religious teachings and practices. Give me the grace and wisdom to repent of and renounce all spiritual counterfeits. In the name of Jesus Christ I pray, amen.

When you've prayed this prayer, you might be surprised what comes to mind. You may remember things you had completely forgotten about, or that you didn't realise were displeasing to Him. Look at what the Bible says on these practices:

> "Do not turn to mediums or seek out spiritists, for you will be defiled by them. I am the LORD your God." Leviticus 19:31

> "I will set my face against anyone who turns to mediums and spiritists to prostitute themselves by following them, and I will cut them off from their people." Leviticus 20:6

> "Let no one be found among you who…practices divination or sorcery, interprets omens, engages in witchcraft, or casts spells, or who is a medium or spiritist or who consults the dead. Anyone who does these things is detestable to the LORD." Deuteronomy 18:10-12a

> "Dear friends, do not believe every spirit, but test the spirits to see whether they are from God, because many false prophets have gone out into the world. This is how you can recognise the Spirit of God: Every spirit that acknowledges that Jesus Christ has come in the flesh is from God, but every spirit that does not acknowledge Jesus is not from God." 1 John 4:1-3

You don't need to turn to other spirits or religions for guidance or healing as God can give you all the guidance and healing you need as you seek Him in prayer. God's healing and guidance is far better and lasting. There are many spirits in this world that are not from God and do us harm. God has some strong words to say on the subject. We often don't realise that getting involved with these practices are harmful to us, but they are. All spirits that are not from God are of Satan. They bring sickness, fear, and lead us away from God. Don't allow evil spirits to deceive you into thinking that they are helpful. They are not. They are deceptive and just open the door to the Devil to afflict us in some way.

I know one woman who had a relationship with a spirit. She would seek guidance from it and allow the spirit to make decisions for her. She enjoyed this relationship but, in the end, it tried to persuade her to commit suicide to be with it, which she didn't want to do. Unclean spirits bring sickness and death into people's lives. These are spirits who once rebelled against God and were thrown out of heaven. They are not good for you! Their guidance will not lead anywhere good. No Christian should be engaging in these practices. Our guidance must come from God alone and through His written Word, led by His Holy Spirit.

You will need to repent and renounce any connection you've had with any of these practices. If someone is not willing to repent and deal with these issues, they cannot continue the process of deliverance until they are. Not much can be done for someone who isn't willing to repent and deal with the issues that prevent them from being set free. Deliverance will be prevented as they are allowing the enemy the right to remain. As I've said, deliverance is not a substitute for repentance. For such a person, pray that they would become willing to repent one day.

If you are willing to repent and close the door to the enemy in your life once and for all, here is a suggested prayer:

Dear heavenly Father, I confess that I have been involved in _____ *(name activity)*. I now repent of that and renounce it as counterfeit. Father God, please forgive me for this sin and fill me with your Holy Spirit. I want to be guided and healed only by You. I command every evil spirit to leave my life and never return in the name of Jesus Christ. Deliver me from the evil one and may your kingdom come, and your will be done in my life I pray, amen.

If you have any digital content, books, teachings, crystals, or other objects from these practices, I strongly encourage you to destroy them and throw them away. Keeping these items will keep a foothold open to the enemy who may tempt you again in the future to pick those items up again. Don't just give them away as someone else may get caught up with them. Destroy them and throw them away. Look at how new converts to Christ dealt with such items in Acts 19:18-20:

> "Many of those who believed now came and openly confessed what they had done. A number who had practiced sorcery brought their scrolls together and burned them publicly. When they calculated the value of the scrolls, the total came to fifty thousand drachmas [one drachma was worth about a day's wage]. In this way the word of the Lord spread widely and grew in power."

Step 5: Command the unclean spirits to leave

As we have looked at before, because of what Jesus Christ accomplished through His death on the cross and His resurrection, we have His designated authority for healing and freedom through deliverance. It's a blessing given to us by grace through faith. We can take hold of the authority that Christ has given us and drive out unclean spirits in His name. *Everything is to be done in the name of Jesus Christ.* It's the only name the Devil will flee from. Place your faith in God and His authoritative Word, which teaches us that the enemy has been defeated:

> "He [Jesus] replied, 'I saw Satan fall like lightning from heaven. I have given you authority to trample on snakes and scorpions and to overcome all the power of the enemy; nothing will harm you. However, do not rejoice that the spirits submit to you, but rejoice that your names are written in heaven.'" Luke 10:18-20

You have authority in Jesus Christ to overcome all the works of the Devil, so let's exercise that.

Praying for deliverance

Now that you have dealt with any issues, it's time to evict those unwanted demonic intruders. Here is a prayer you can use:

In the authority of the name of the Lord Jesus Christ, you evil spirit(s), I rebuke you and command you to leave my life and never return. You have no right to remain and so I command you to come out. Leave my life right now in the almighty name of Jesus Christ. Heavenly Father, deliver me from the evil one and may your kingdom come, and your will be done in my life. I also ask you to heal me completely of every work of the enemy, and for all pain to be removed. Fill my whole life with your Holy Spirit I pray. Thank you so much for your freedom and healing in Christ's all-powerful name, amen.

If you have the gift of praying in tongues, pray in the Holy Spirit. When you allow God's Holy Spirit to pray through you during deliverance, it significantly speeds up the process. I find praying in tongues for deliverance very effective and I recommend it.

When an unclean spirit is leaving, you may not experience anything at all as it does, or you may experience breathlessness, yawning, a crying out, or coughing. This is normal and will quickly pass.

Praying for others

You can use the same prayer to pray for others. If you do, always keep your eyes open so you are aware of what's going on. I recommend asking another person to join the prayer time for safeguarding reasons and to offer support and pray quietly in the background. Go through all the steps with the person you're praying for to make sure all issues are dealt with and all doors to the enemy are closed.

Where there is a greater stronghold of the enemy in someone's life, the person you are praying for may have an unfocussed gaze, incoherent talk or even become somewhat aggressive. If you find that the unclean spirit is being disruptive, take authority over it and bind it by saying, *"In the name of Jesus Christ, be bound / be quiet / be still."* Command it to be quiet and sit down if the person is restless or distracting.

You might find it helpful to say out loud some helpful scriptures during the process, reminding the enemy of his defeat:

> "No weapon formed against you shall prosper..." Isaiah 54:17a (NKJV)

> "You are of God, little children, and have overcome them, because He who is in you is greater than he who is in the world." 1 John 4:4 (NKJV)

Again, if you can pray in tongues, do so. Evil spirits *have to* surrender to Christ.

Finally

Your life will feel so different now once any spiritual intruders are commanded to leave. God will fill you with His peace and will release His healing. Please remember, it is of utmost importance that you continue to walk with God to maintain your freedom and continue to grow in God. Spend time with God every day, reading the Bible and in prayer. Seek to develop your relationship with God. There are many great books and phone apps out there to help you. Life with God is exciting and adventurous, and God has a wonderful plan for your life. Continue to seek God for prayer is powerful. There is nothing God cannot do!

Questions for further study

1. Why do you think it displeases God when people turn to guidance from ungodly spirits in their life?

2. Read Exodus 8:16-19. What did Moses do that the magicians could not? What was the opinion of the magicians?

3. Please read Isaiah 2:6. Why did God abandon His people in this verse?

4. Now read Galatians 5:16-26. What do you learn from these verses about the kind of life God wants us to live?

5. Please read John 8:36. What does this Bible verse promise?

6. Now read Galatians 5:13-14. What are we encouraged to do with our freedom in Christ?

7. Has God spoken to you through this chapter about an issue you may need to pray and address? Take some time now to pray to God about that and ask Him to heal you and set you free.

Chapter 12

For yours is the kingdom and the power and the glory forever

Have you noticed that the Lord's Prayer begins and ends with acknowledging and praying for God's kingdom?

"In this manner, therefore pray: Our Father in heaven, hallowed be your name. *Your kingdom come.* Your will be done on earth as it is in heaven. Give us this day our daily bread. And forgive us our debts, as we forgive our debtors. And do not lead us into temptation but deliver us from the evil one. *For Yours is the kingdom and the power and the glory forever.* Amen." Matthew 6:9-13 (NKJV – author's emphasis)

In chapter five, we looked at what the kingdom of God is and what it means to pray for God's kingdom to come and for God's will to be done here on earth. In this chapter, we will broaden our view and look at the eternal and eschatological aspect of God's kingdom.

Jesus Christ is coming a second time to earth

As you read the book of Revelation in the Bible, you come to understand that God has dramatic plans of intervention in our world and that one day, evil and injustice will be dealt with, once and for all, by God. This ushering in of God's eternal plans centre around the return to earth of our Lord and Saviour Jesus Christ. This time, Christ's coming won't be in a humble stable surrounded by animals, but will be powerful and glorious surrounded by angels and visible by everyone:

> "For as lightning that comes from the east is visible even in the west, so will be the coming of the Son of Man… Then will appear the sign of the Son of Man in heaven. And then all the peoples of the earth will mourn when they see the Son of Man coming on the clouds of heaven, with power and great glory. And he will send his angels with a loud trumpet call, and they will gather his elect from the four winds, from one end of the heavens to the other." Matthew 24:27, 30-31

The Son of Man Jesus is referring to in these verses is Himself and everyone will see Him and His glory when He returns. The Bible explains that there are a number of reasons for His return. Firstly, Jesus Christ is returning to gather His people, those alive and those sleeping in death, to Himself:

> "For the Lord himself will come down from heaven, with a loud command, with the voice of the archangel and with the trumpet call of God, and the dead in Christ will rise first. After that, we who are still alive and are left will be caught up together with them in the clouds to meet the Lord in the air. And so we will be with the Lord forever." 1 Thessalonians 4:16-17

As believers, we live with the hope of eternal life with God. Physical death is not the end for us for this life here on earth is but a small foretaste of the life to come. We are to live our time on earth forging our relationship with God and for God's kingdom purposes, all of which prepare us for eternity with God. Jesus Christ is coming back for His followers and we need to be ready for we do not know when that day will come as Jesus explained:

> "For the in the days before the flood, people were eating and drinking, marrying and giving in marriage, up to the day Noah entered the ark; and they knew nothing about what would happen until the flood came and took them all away. That is how it will be at the coming of the Son of Man. Two men will be in the field; one will be taken and the other left. Two women will be grinding with a hand mill; one will be taken and the other left." Matthew 24:38-41

Although we do not know the day of Jesus' return, we are called to live wisely and productively in the light of its anticipation. Now is the time to put our lives right before God and make His kingdom priorities ours.

A second reason Jesus Christ is coming back is to usher in God's judgment on the earth. Whoever we are, we will all have to appear before Christ's throne and give an account for how we have lived our lives, whether for good or for evil:

> "When the Son of Man comes in his glory and all the angels with him, he will sit on his glorious throne. All the nations will be gathered before him, and he will separate the people one from another as a shepherd separates the sheep from the goats. He will put the sheep on his right and the goats on his left.
> Then the King will say to those on his right, 'Come, you who are blessed by my Father; take your inheritance, the kingdom prepared for you since the creation of the

world. For I was hungry and you gave me something to eat, I was thirsty and you gave me something to drink, I was a stranger and you invited me in, I needed clothes and you clothed me, I was sick and you looked after me, I was in prison and you came to visit me….whatever you did for one of the least of these brothers and sisters of mine, you did for me.
Then he will say to those on his left, 'Depart from me, you who are cursed, into the eternal fire prepared for the Devil and his angels. For I was hungry and you gave me nothing to eat, I was thirsty and you gave me nothing to drink, I was a stranger and you did not invite me in, I needed clothes and you did not clothe me, I was sick and in prison and you did not look after me.'" Matthew 25:1-31-36, 40-43

For those people who have done evil, they will be judged. The fact that we will all have to give an account to Christ is a very sobering reality and should encourage us to fulfil the command of Jesus in Matthew 6:33 to seek first God's kingdom and His righteousness.

God will deal with Satan and evil once and for all

God will deal with Satan once and for all one day. He is doomed, a fate you can read about in the book of Revelation. This unique book is filled with prophetic words and dramatic images of apocalyptic scenes and events still to come. Yet its message is clear: God is far greater than the Devil and God will eventually dispose of him and his evil minions, casting them into the lake of fire and brimstone where they will forever be tormented:

> "And the Devil, who deceived them, was thrown into the lake of burning sulphur, where the beast and the false

prophet had been thrown. They will be tormented day and night for ever and ever." Revelation 20:10

This is the future of the Devil: tormented day and night for ever and ever, whilst God and His people will enjoy God's wonderful kingdom, power and glory for ever and ever. The Devil knows his future, which is why he is at work to destroy as many of God's children as he can. However, for God and His people, our future is so blessed as we will be with God in a new heavens and earth, for ever and ever:

> "Then I saw a new heaven and a new earth, for the first heaven and the first earth had passed away, and there was no longer any sea. I saw the Holy City, the new Jerusalem, coming down out of heaven from God, prepared as a bride beautifully dressed for her husband. And I heard a loud voice from the throne saying, 'Look! God's dwelling place is now among the people, and he will dwell with them. They will be his people, and God himself will be with them and be their God. He will wipe every tear from their eyes. There will be no more death or mourning or crying or pain, for the old order of things has passed away.'" Revelation 21:1-4

What a wonderful future awaits those who trust in Jesus Christ as their Lord and Saviour. Understand what lies in store for you: dwelling with God for ever in heaven. It will be so beautiful and glorious, beyond our understanding. There will be no more tears or death or mourning or pain, and we will see God in all His glory and power:

> "Then the angel showed me the river of the water of life, as clear as crystal, flowing from the throne of God and of the Lamb down the middle of the great street of the city. On each side of the river stood the tree of life bearing

twelve crops of fruit, yielding its fruit every month. And the leaves of the tree are for the healing of the nations. No longer will there be any curse. The throne of God and of the Lamb will be in the city, and his servants will serve him. They will see his face, and his name will be on their foreheads. There will be no more night. They will not need the light of a lamp or the light of the sun, for the Lord God will give them light. And they will reign for ever and ever." Revelation 22:1-5.

The kingdom and the power and the glory belong to God for ever and ever. Look forward to your incredible eternity!

PART C

Questions for further study

1. Read John 5:24. What does Jesus promise in this verse for the person who follows Christ's words?

2. What does Romans 6:23 teach us about the gift of God?

3. Now read 1 John 5:13. What does God want us to know and be confident of? How does that knowledge affect you?

4. What does Galatians 6:8 teach us about the importance of how we live our lives?

5. According to John 3:36, where is eternal life found?

6. According to John 17:3, what does eternal life look like?

7. What does 1 John 2:25 teach us about what God has promised us? How does that make you feel?

Chapter 13

Continue to grow in God

"The LORD said, 'I have indeed seen the misery of my people in Egypt. I have heard them crying out because of their slave drivers, and I am concerned about their suffering. So I have come down to rescue them from the hand of the Egyptians and to bring them up out of that land into a good and spacious land, a land flowing with milk and honey." Exodus 3:7-8

Don't look back

The Israelites had suffered so much during the four centuries they had been in Egypt. Their Egyptian masters had made them slaves, forcing them to endure harsh working conditions, punishing them cruelly. They hated their circumstances and suffered so much that they eventually cried out to God to rescue them.

God answered them and called Moses to lead them out of slavery and into a new and bountiful land. God did what He said He would do, and brought them out of Egypt with astonishing miracles by His powerful hand, which even the Egyptians came to fear and respect. However, a journey to the promised land which should have taken a matter of weeks ended up taking forty long years because of their disobedience and distrust of God. Instead of being grateful for God's dramatic deliverance and trusting His ongoing provisions, they grumbled and complained before Him, eventually incurring His judgment:

> "Now the people complained about their hardships in the hearing of the LORD, and when he heard them his anger was aroused…The rabble with them began to crave other food, and again the Israelites started wailing and said, 'If only we had meat to eat! We remember the fish we ate in Egypt at no cost – also the cucumbers, melons, leeks, onions and garlic. But now we have lost our appetite; we never see anything but this manna!'" Numbers 11:1, 4-6

For the sake of food, they began looking back to Egypt, forgetting how they had been brutally treated. A daily diet of miraculous manna had stirred up frustration, but instead of asking God to provide more with a simple heart of gratitude and trust, they complained. Of course God wasn't expecting them to live permanently on a diet of manna, but their attitude and heart towards God just wasn't right. God gave them the meat they craved, but they also found themselves under judgment.

The Israelites are not alone in making the mistake of foolishly looking back. When Sodom and Gomorrah's sin became just too wicked, God destroyed them, but not before rescuing and protecting Lot and his family. As God's angels brought them out, they gave them these simple instructions:

> "As soon as they had brought them out, one of them said, 'Flee for your lives! Don't look back, and don't stop anywhere in the plain! Flee to the mountains or you will be swept away!" Genesis 19:17

The instructions were clear: flee, don't stop and don't look back. However, Lot's wife didn't listen and reaped the consequences for her poor decision:

> "But Lot's wife looked back, and she became a pillar of salt." Genesis 19:26

It's so important that once you have received freedom from God that you don't nostalgically look back to those past bondages, relationships and circumstances that once caused you harm. Looking back causes you to take our eyes off the present blessings of God and the wonderful future that God wants to lead you into. It can also stir back up harmful desires that led you into bondage in the first place. God's blessings are always conditional upon our trust and obedience as the Israelites found. So be wise in your daily decisions.

Remember, Satan is the father of lies and lying is his native language (John 8:44). Everything he whispers to you is *not true* and is designed to defeat and destroy you. Don't listen to the deception and condemnation of the enemy of your soul. As Romans 8:1-2 declare,

> "There is now no condemnation for those who are in Christ Jesus, because through Christ Jesus the law of the Spirit who gives life has set you free from the law of sin and death."

Friend, you have been set free and are dearly loved by God. You are more than a conqueror in Christ:

> "If God is for us, who can be against us? He who did not spare his own Son, but gave him up for us all – how will he not also, along with him, graciously give us all things?...Who shall separate us from the love of Christ? Shall trouble or hardship or persecution or famine or

nakedness or danger or sword?... No, in all these things we are more than conquerors through him who loved us. For I am convinced that neither death nor life, neither angels nor demons, neither the present nor the future, nor any powers, neither height nor depth, nor anything else in all creation, will be able to separate us from the love of God that is in Christ Jesus our Lord.'" Romans 8:31-32, 35, 37-39

Nothing can separate you from God's love. Remember the words of Jeremiah 29:11 and put your hope in God and trust Him for the good future He has for you. As you trust in Him, He will guide you and bring wonderful blessings into your life, far better than anything you could have imagined or done for yourself.

Walk in the armour of God

Another important thing to remember in maintaining your freedom is to invest in your ongoing spiritual growth and protection. This will not come by itself. You need to make wise choices and spend time on those spiritual activities that will continue to build your faith and deepen your relationship with God.

> "[A]nyone who competes as an athlete does not receive the victor's crown except by competing according to the rules."

Every athlete understands the importance of investing in a training programme and perseverance. People do not become athletes by being indifferent or undisciplined. Those who win races and tournaments have invested many hours of training prior to their wins and compete according to the rules.

Everything in life that's of some worth or value takes a portion of our time and effort in terms of investment. If you want to succeed in a career, learn how to drive a car, achieve weight loss goals, play in instrument, or be a good partner, they all require some level of commitment and input.

It's no different in your relationship with God. To develop your faith, you need to devote some time and effort. To grow in God, set aside time each day and invest in spiritual disciplines that will strengthen your faith and protect your freedom. As we've looked at previously, we have the armour of God, things we can do and implement to strengthen and protect us: walking in *truth, righteousness, readiness, faith, confidence of salvation, the Word of God and praying in the Holy Spirit* (Ephesians 6). These are our tools and weapons for our ongoing protection and growth and are most powerful and helpful for growing in God.

Devote yourself to prayer and read and obey God's Word. Walk in faith, truth and righteousness. You will not grow in God any other way. If you have done deliverance prayer, this is even more important as you need to fill that area of your life with God's Holy Spirit to safeguard it from reoccupation.

There are no substitutes for the essentials of regularly reading the Bible and prayer.

There are no alternatives for these spiritual disciplines. Ground yourself in the meat and soundness of God's Word. Build the foundation of your life on obedience to the truth of the Bible. It will anchor you. How else will you know what God's will is for your life, or how God is guiding you?

> "So then, just as you received Christ Jesus as Lord, continue to live your lives in him, rooted and built up in him, strengthened in the faith as you were taught, and overflowing with thankfulness." Colossians 2:6-7

As you spend time with God in His Word and prayer, you will experience God speaking to you, guiding and encouraging you. I love spending time with God at the start of my day as it puts me in a good frame of mind, gives me peace and hope, and protects my heart from fear and worry. Spending time with God each day will be a huge blessing to your life as you offload your worries and burdens to Him in prayer and see the Creator of the universe answer you.

As we have seen in our time together in this book, prayer is the most effective and powerful thing you can do because it moves God, and when God moves, wonderful things happen. If Jesus Christ felt the need to spend time in prayer with His Father, how much more should we? Spending time with God in prayer each day, asking for His help and provision, is a far more effective use of your time than spending time worrying and fretting. Use the Lord's Prayer as a template.

God wants you to know and experience Him as your loving and faithful Heavenly Father. There is no greater blessing than walking through life with the Creator of the heavens and earth and experiencing His help and miraculous interventions. It's exciting and adventurous!

As you read God's Word daily, your spiritual nourishment, you will grow and flourish. We need God's truth more than ever in today's generation. If you don't feed yourself, you will soon find your faith waning. Don't make that mistake:

> "Keep this Book of the Law always on your lips; meditate on it day and night, so that you may be careful to do everything written in it. Then you will be prosperous and successful." Joshua 1:8

God's Word is like a compass, guiding us and bringing our hearts and minds back to truth and sense. The alternative is worry, fear, and confusion, which never accomplish anything profitable:

> "The seed that fell among thorns stands for those who hear, but as they go on their way they are choked by life's worries, riches and pleasures, and they do not mature. But the seed on good soil stands for those with a noble and good heart, *who hear the word, retain it, and by persevering produce a crop.*" Luke 8:14-15 (italics mine)

The Bible is full of promises of God. Find a verse that suits your need and stand on it. Pray about it and tell God you're trusting Him in faith to fulfil that in your life. That's a powerful way to walk with God and He loves that kind of bold faith. If more people took God at His Word, we'd see a lot more miracles and divine interventions. God's Word and prayer are powerful. Do you need a job, healing, guidance or financial help? Then pray and stand on the promises of God. As you do, God will guide you and you will receive your answer.

If you think you're too busy to pray, then you're probably too busy to not pray. Your days will go much smoother and your heart will be filled with much more peace and strength if you will set aside a time each day to bring your needs before our all-powerful God. Prayer will protect your heart from anxiety and stress, and as you see God move in response to your prayers, you will grow in faith and in your understanding of who He is and how He really feels about you. Prayer is a far more productive use of your time compared to spending time worrying, which Jesus said is just a waste of time (Matthew 6:25ff).

Find the time that works best for you. Personally, I'm a morning person so I get up early before the house is awake, to spend time with God. It's the most important time of the day for me. I love spending that quiet time with God each day. It gives me the opportunity to offload on to God what's on my heart and to receive His input. He invites us all to come to Him and give Him our burdens:

> "Come to me, all you who are weary and burdened, and I will give you rest. Take my yoke upon you and learn from me, for I am gentle and humble in heart, and you will find rest for your souls. For my yoke is easy and my burden is light." Matthew 11:28-30

Prioritise your divine appointment with God. When you allow Him to guide you, you will find that God's purposes are far greater than any you can come up with. God knows and understands you better than you know yourself, and He knows how you function best and what will bring you joy. You can completely trust your life into His hands. I made that decision in my late teens, and I've never looked back. God is so faithful.

If you will do what Jesus said by seeking first God's kingdom and righteousness, your Heavenly Father promises to take care of your practical needs. If you trust Him with all your heart, He promises to guide you. One of my favourite Bible verses is found in Proverbs 3:5-6, which has been so helpful to me over the years:

> "Trust in the LORD with all your heart and lean not on your own understanding; in all your ways submit to him, and he will make your paths straight."

We often don't know what is going to happen from one day to the next, but God does. He understands everything and sees the future, so it's wise to trust Him and rest in Him rather trying to work things out ourselves.

The Bible does not promise that we will never experience trials and tribulations. After all, we live in a fallen world with evil forces at work. However, God does promise that He will protect and help us through the storms and bring us through to victory. Whilst I have found following God to be an exciting adventure at times, there have of course been painful moments too. But I have also found that God was right there, guiding me through those painful times, bringing me much needed comfort, strength and hope. He will do the same for you.

Whatever needs we have, He can meet them as we turn to Him. We all go through challenging and painful moments in life, but life is so much better when you walk with God and trust Him to bring you through to victory. As Proverbs 3 explains, we need to trust God with all our hearts and not rely on our own very limited understanding of things. As we do these things and submit to God, He will do His part and guide us and bring us through.

Never give up

Someone once asked the question: how long should we keep praying for something? Until God answers. Some prayers seem to be answered quickly, whilst others can take time. The key is to never give up praying for something if the answer seems a long time in coming. I have found that where a change of heart is needed, perseverance in prayer is often required. God is always at work even though we may not see it yet. In Luke 11:5-10, Jesus encouraged us to persevere in prayer:

> "Suppose you have a friend, and you go to him at midnight and say, 'Friend, lend me three loaves of bread; a friend of mine on a journey has come to me, and I have no food to offer him,' And suppose the one inside answers, 'Don't bother me. The door is already locked, and my children and I are in bed. I can't get up

and give you anything,' I tell you, even though he will not get up and give you the bread because of friendship, yet because of your shameless audacity he wills surely get up and give you as much as you need.

So I say to you: Ask and it will be given to you; seek and you will find; knock and the door will be opened to you. For everyone who asks receives; the one who seeks finds, and to the one who knocks, the door will be opened."

There's no need to be timid in prayer. In this parable, it was the person who went beyond social protocol and shamelessly bothered his friend until he answered who got what he needed. Jesus encouraged us to ask, seek and knock God's door. God promises that we will receive what we ask for, find what we're looking for and doors will open. What a promise. Don't give up praying.

Specific prayers bring specific answers. Seeing God answer your prayers will strengthen your faith and encourage you to trust God for more. It is a great blessing to be able to bring our needs and requests to our loving and faithful Heavenly Father who promises to answer us. Your prayers can change your life, your family, your nation and the world. Prayer is so powerful. Every day I pray:

> *"Heavenly Father, please provide my daily needs, lead me away from temptation and deliver me from the evil one. May your kingdom come, and your will be done in my life, marriage, family, work, and church as it is in heaven. In the name of Jesus Christ I pray."*

I encourage you to do that same. May you continue to grow in God and see Him do great things through your prayers! Amen.

PART C

Questions for further study

1. Now that you have finished reading this book, why would you say prayer is important in your own words? What are some of the benefits of prayer?

2. Read Luke 5:16. Why do you think Jesus went to isolated places to pray?

3. Please read Luke 22:32. Who did Jesus pray for in this verse? What did He pray for exactly and why?

4. Read Matthew 6:5-8. What can we learn about how prayer should be done from these verses?

5. Please read Matthew 6:25-34. What does Jesus promise God will do for the person who will seek God's kingdom and His righteousness first?

6. Have you ever had an answer to prayer? What was that?

7. What stood out from this book the most for you?

Appendix

31 Days of Bible Verses for Healing

Allow God's Word to develop the faith you need for you miracle. As you read, ask God by His Holy Spirit to speak to your heart. Pray and ask God to bring healing into your life, and God will answer your prayers. Be specific when you pray.

Day 1 - **Psalm 103:2–5**

Praise the LORD, O my soul, and forget not all his benefits— who forgives all your sins and heals all your diseases, who redeems your life from the pit and crowns you with love and compassion, who satisfies your desires with good things so that your youth is renewed like the eagle's.

Day 2 - **Mark 11: 23 to 24**

Truly, I say to you, whoever says to this mountain, 'Be taken up and thrown into the sea,' and does not doubt in his heart, but believes that what he says will come to pass, it will be done for him. Therefore I tell you, whatever you ask in prayer, believe that you have received it, and it will be yours.

Day 3 – **Psalm 107:19 - 21**

Then they cried to the LORD in their trouble, and he saved them from their distress. He sent out his word and healed them; he rescued them from the grave. Let them give thanks to the LORD for his unfailing love and his wonderful deeds for mankind.

Day 4 - **Matthew 9:35**

And Jesus went throughout all the cities and villages, teaching in their synagogues and proclaiming the gospel of the kingdom and healing every disease and every affliction.

Day 5 - **Luke 6: 17 to 19**

And he came down with them and stood on a level place, with a great crowd of his disciples and a great multitude of people from all Judea and Jerusalem and the seacoast of Tyre and Sidon, who came to hear him and to be healed of their diseases. And those who were troubled with unclean spirits were cured. And all the crowd sought to touch him, for power came out from him and healed them all.

Day 6 - **Matthew 9:28–30a**

When he had gone indoors, the blind men came to him, and he asked them, "Do you believe that I am able to do this?" "Yes, Lord." they replied. Then he touched their eyes and said, "According to your faith will it be done to you"; and their sight was restored.

Day 7 - **Jeremiah 17: 14**

Heal me, O Lord, and I shall be healed; save me, and I shall be saved, for you are my praise.

Day 8 - **John 5: 6 to 9**

When Jesus saw him lying there and learned that he had been in this condition for a long time, he asked him, "Do you want to get well?" "Sir," the invalid replied, "I have no one to help me into the pool when the water is stirred. While I am trying to get in, someone else goes down ahead of me." Then Jesus said to him, "Get up! Pick up your mat and walk." At once the man was cured; he picked up his mat and walked.

Day 9 - **Luke 10: 17 to 19**

The seventy-two returned with joy, saying, "Lord, even the demons are subject to us in your name!" And he said to them, "I saw Satan fall like lightning from heaven. Behold, I have given you authority to tread on serpents and scorpions, and over all the power of the enemy, and nothing shall hurt you.

Day 10 - **John 14:12 to 14:**

"I tell you the truth, anyone who believes in me will do the same works I have done, and even greater works, because I am going to be with the Father. You can ask for anything in my name, and I will do it, so that the Son can bring glory to the Father. Yes, ask me for anything in my name, and I will do it!

Day 11 - **James 5:13-15**

Are any of you suffering hardships? You should pray. Are any of you happy? You should sing praises. Are any of you sick? You should call for the elders of the church to come and pray over you, anointing you with oil in the name of the Lord. Such a prayer offered in faith will heal the sick, and the Lord will make you well.

Day 12 - **Isaiah 53:4-5** (KJV with footnotes)**:**

Surely he hath borne our griefs (sicknesses) and carried our sorrows (pains): yet we did esteem him stricken, smitten of God, and afflicted. But he was wounded for our transgressions, he was bruised for our iniquities: the chastisement of our peace was upon him; and with his stripes we are healed.
Compare these verses with *Matthew 8:14 to 17 below which is based on Isaiah 53: 4-5:*

Matthew 8: 14 to 17

When Jesus came into Peter's house, he saw Peter's mother-in-law lying in bed with a fever. He touched her hand and the fever left her, and she got up and began to wait on him. When evening came, many who were demon-possessed were brought to him, and he drove out the spirits with a word and healed all the sick. This was to fulfil what was spoken through the prophet Isaiah: "He took up our infirmities and bore our diseases."

Day 13 - **Exodus 15:26**

He said, 'If you listen carefully to the Lord your God and do what is right in his eyes, if you pay attention to his commands and keep all his decrees, I will not bring on you any of the diseases I brought on the Egyptians, for I am the Lord, who heals you.'

Day 14 - **1 John 3:8b**

The reason the Son of God appeared was to destroy the Devil's work.

APPENDIX

Day 15 - **Mark 5: 28 to 34**

For she said, "If I touch even his garments, I will be made well." And immediately the flow of blood dried up, and she felt in her body that she was healed of her disease. And Jesus, perceiving in himself that power had gone out from him, immediately turned about in the crowd and said, "Who touched my garments?" And his disciples said to him, "You see the crowd pressing around you, and yet you say, 'Who touched me?'" And he looked around to see who had done it. But the woman, knowing what had happened to her, came in fear and trembling and fell down before him and told him the whole truth. And he said to her, "Daughter, your faith has made you well; go in peace, and be healed of your disease."

Day 16 - **Exodus 23:25-26**

Worship the Lord your God, and his blessing will be on your food and water. I will take away disease from among you, and none will miscarry or be barren in your land. I will give you a full life span.

Day 17 - **1 Samuel 1:10-11 and 19-20**

In her deep anguish Hannah prayed to the LORD, weeping bitterly. And she made a vow, saying, "LORD Almighty, if you will only look on your servant's misery and remember me, and not forget your servant but give her a son, then I will give him to the LORD for all the days of his life, and no razor will ever be used on his head."
Early the next morning they arose and worshipped before the LORD and then went back to their home at Ramah. Elkanah made love to his wife Hannah, and the LORD remembered her. So in the course of time Hannah became pregnant and gave birth to a son. She named him Samuel, saying, "Because I asked the LORD for him."

Day 18 - **Psalm 30:1-2:**

I will exalt you, Lord, for you lifted me out of the depths and did not let my enemies gloat over me. Lord my God, I called to you for help, and you healed me.

Day 19 - **Psalm 146:8**

The Lord sets the prisoners free; the Lord opens the eyes of the blind. The Lord lifts up those who are bowed down; the Lord loves the righteous.

Day 20 – **Proverbs 4: 20 - 22**

My son, pay attention to what I say; turn your ear to my words. Do not let them out of your sight, keep them within your heart; for they are life to those who find them and health to one's whole body.

Day 21 – **Matthew 4:23 – 24**

Jesus went through Galilee, teaching in their synagogues, proclaiming the good news of the kingdom, and healing every disease and sickness among the people. News about him spread all over Syria, and people brought to him all who were ill with various diseases, those suffering severe pain, the demon-possessed, those having seizures, and the paralyzed; and he healed them.

Day 22 – **Luke 4: 17 - 21**

The scroll of the prophet Isaiah was handed to him. Unrolling it, he found the place where it is written: "The Spirit of the Lord is on me, because he has anointed me to proclaim good news to the poor. He has sent me to proclaim freedom for the prisoners and recovery of sight for the blind, to set the oppressed free, to proclaim the year of the

Lord's favour." Then he rolled up the scroll, gave it back to the attendant and sat down. The eyes of everyone in the synagogue were fastened on him. He began by saying to them, "Today this scripture is fulfilled in your hearing."

Day 23 – **1 Peter 2:24**

"He himself bore our sins" in his body on the cross, so that we might die to sins and live for righteousness; "by his wounds you have been healed."

Day 24 – **Psalm 41:3 - 4**

The LORD sustains him on their sickbed and restores them from their bed of illness. I said, "Have mercy on me, LORD; heal me, for I have sinned against you."

Day 25 – **Psalm 147:3**

He heals the brokenhearted and binds up their wounds.

Day 26 – **Hebrews 11:1** (NKJV)

Now faith is the substance of things hoped for, the evidence of things not seen.

Day 27 – **Jeremiah 30:17**

For I will restore health to you, and your wounds I will heal, declares the LORD.

Day 28 – **Isaiah 38:16 – 19**

You restored me to health and let me live. Surely it was for my benefit that I suffered such anguish. In your love you kept me from the pit of destruction; you have put all my sins behind your back. For the grave cannot praise you, death cannot sing your praise; those who go down to the pit cannot hope for your faithfulness. The living, the living – they praise you, as I am doing today; parents tell their children about your faithfulness.

Day 29 – **Psalm 41: 1 to 4**

Blessed are those who have regard for the weak; the LORD delivers them in times of trouble. The LORD protects and preserves them – they are counted among the blessed in the land – he does not give them over to the desire of their foes. The LORD sustains them on their sickbed and restores them from their bed of illness. I said, "Have mercy on me, LORD; heal me, for I have sinned against you."

Day 30 - **Psalm 6:1 - 2**

LORD, do not rebuke me in your anger or discipline me in your wrath. Have mercy on me, LORD, for I am faint; heal me, LORD, for my bones are in agony.

Day 31 - **Isaiah 58:6 – 8**

"Is this not the kind of fasting I have chosen: to loose the chains of injustice and untie the cords of the yoke, to set the oppressed free and break every yoke? Is it not to share your food with the hungry and to provide the poor wanderer with shelter – when you see the naked, to clothe them, and not to turn away from your own flesh and blood? Then your light will break forth like the dawn, and your healing will quickly appear; then your righteousness will go before you, and the glory of the LORD will be your rear guard."

Additional recommended reading

Blessing or Curse: You can choose by Derek Prince

The Steps to Freedom in Christ: A Biblical Guide to Help You Resolve Personal and Spiritual Conflicts and Become a Fruitful Disciple of Christ by Dr Neil T. Anderson

Jesus – Healer & Deliverer by Peter Horrobin

They Shall Expel Demons by Derek Prince

Running with God: A Discipleship Guide to Grow in Faith and Experience the Love and Power of God by Liz Hill O'Shea

The Nature of Faith and Miracles by Liz Hill O'Shea

Printed in Great Britain
by Amazon